T0278250

THE THREE KINGDOMS OF KOREA

LOST CIVILIZATIONS

The books in this series explore the rise and fall of the great civilizations and peoples of the ancient world. Each book considers not only their history but their art, culture and lasting legacy and asks why they remain important and relevant in our world today.

Already published:

The Aztecs Frances F. Berdan
The Barbarians Peter Bogucki
Egypt Christina Riggs
The Etruscans Lucy Shipley
The Goths David M. Gwynn
The Greeks Philip Matyszak
The Hittites Damien Stone
The Inca Kevin Lane
The Indus Andrew Robinson
The Maya Megan E. O'Neil
Nubia Sarah M. Schellinger
The Persians Geoffrey Parker and Brenda Parker
The Phoenicians Vadim S. Jigoulov
The Sumerians Paul Collins
The Three Kingdoms of Korea Richard D. McBride II

THE THREE KINGDOMS OF KOREA

LOST CIVILIZATIONS

RICHARD D. MCBRIDE II

REAKTION BOOKS

To David and Sean
My two talented hwarang

Published by Reaktion Books Ltd
Unit 32, Waterside
44–48 Wharf Road
London N1 7UX, UK
www.reaktionbooks.co.uk

First published 2024

Printed and bound in India by Replika Press Pvt. Ltd

A catalogue record for this book is available from the British Library

ISBN 978 1 78914 875 6

CONTENTS

Chronology

2333 BCE	Legendary birth of Tan'gun
10th cen. BCE	Bronze Age starts in Northeast Asia
8th–7th cen. BCE	Founding of Old Chosŏn polity
c. 700 BCE	Iron Culture starts
194 BCE	Wiman (Wei Man) usurps throne in Old Chosŏn
109	Han China attacks Old Chosŏn
108	Han China conquers Old Chosŏn, establishes Lelang, Zhenfan and Lintun commanderies
107	Han China establishes the Xuantu commandery
82	Han China closes Zhenfan and Lintun commanderies and redistributes land to Lelang and Xuantu commanderies
75	Koguryŏ attacks Xuantu commandery; Xuantu commandery removed to Liaodong region
57	Silla: birth of legendary founder Pak Hyŏkkŏse
37	Koguryŏ: Chumong leaves Puyŏ and founds Koguryŏ
18	Paekche: legendary founder, King Onjo, ascends throne in Wiryesŏng
3 CE	Koguryŏ moves capital to Kungnaesŏng (present-day Ji'an)
28/42	Kaya: birth of legendary founder, King Suro
146	Koguryŏ raids Xi'anping in the Han commandery of Liaodong, kills the governor of

	Daifang commandery and captures the wife and child of the governor of Lelang commandery
165	Koguryŏ king Ch'adae is assassinated, and his younger brother King Sindae ascends throne
172	Koguryŏ attacks invading force of the Later Han at Chwawŏn
192	Koguryŏ: Chwagaryŏ mobilizes forces and attacks the capital because of corrupt and chaotic rule; Ŭlp'aso recommended to assume the role of counsellor of state
206	Gongsun Kang of Wei divides the southern part of Lelang commandery and establishes Daifang commandery
220	Han dynasty ends; Three Kingdoms period of China begins
242	Koguryŏ strikes Xi'anping in Liaodong commandery
259	Koguryŏ defeats invading Wei Chinese army in Yangmaek valley
285	Puyŏ weakened by an attack from Xianbei
300	Koguryŏ: Minister of State Ch'angjori raises a rebellion, dethrones king and installs Mich'ŏn on throne
311	Koguryŏ seizes Xi'anping in Liaodong commandery
313	Koguryŏ destroys Lelang commandery
314	Koguryŏ strikes and conquers Daifang commandery
331	Koguryŏ king Mich'ŏn dies and King Kogugwŏn ascends the throne
339	Koguryŏ: Murong Huang sacks Sinsŏng and Koguryŏ seeks peaceful settlement
342	Koguryŏ: Murong Huang attacks Hwando Fortress, digs up the Tomb of King Mich'ŏn and takes the mother of the king as hostage

346	Murong Huang destroys Puyŏ state and takes 50,000 people prisoner
356	Silla: legendary *maripkan* Naemul ascends throne
357	Koguryŏ: *The Great Procession* painted in Anak Tomb no. 3
369	Paekche invades Koguryŏ, sacks Ch'iyang Fortress and attacks P'yŏngyang; production of the Seven-Branched Sword
371	Paekche attacks P'yŏngyang; King Kogugwŏn dies in battle
372	Koguryŏ: Buddhism is officially accepted as a state religion, gifted by Former Qin emperor Fu Jian through the efforts of the monk Sundo (Shundao); State University established
373	Koguryŏ promulgates legal and penal code
375	Paekche: Ko Hŭng first compiles documentary records of Paekche court
377	Silla sends emissaries to Former Qin; first appearance of name 'Silla' in Chinese materials
384	Paekche: Buddhism is officially accepted as a state religion, gifted by Eastern Jin dynasty through the efforts of the Indian monk Maranant'a
391	Koguryŏ king Kwanggaet'o ascends throne
392	Silla sends Silsŏng to Koguryŏ as a hostage
396	Koguryŏ king Kwanggaet'o leads navy in assault on Paekche taking 58 fortresses, closes in on Paekche capital; Paekche surrenders and the king's younger brother taken as hostage
400	Koguryŏ: 50,000 troops subdue the combined forces of Paekche, Kaya and Wa to save Silla
402	Silla concludes amicable relations with Wa; Silla prince Misahŭn sent to Wa as hostage
412	Silla sends Pukho to Koguryŏ as hostage

413	Koguryŏ king Kwanggaet'o dies; King Changsu ascends throne
417	Silla: Nulch'i kills King Silsŏng and ascends throne
427	Koguryŏ moves capital from Kungnaesŏng (Ji'an) to P'yŏngyang; builds Anhak Palace
475	Koguryŏ king Changsu conquers Paekche capital at Hansŏng (present-day Seoul)
475	Paekche king Munju ascends throne, moves capital to Ungjin
477	Paekche: Haegu murders King Munju
494	Koguryŏ completely absorbs Puyŏ
502	Silla king Chijŭng prohibits the burial of the living with the dead, institutes the use of oxen in farming
503	Silla officially adopts the name 'Silla'
505	Silla first stores ice and regulates shipping
509	Silla establishes Eastern Market in the capital
510	Paekche king Muryŏng orders strengthening of river embankments and return of vagabonds to farming
517	Silla king Pŏphŭng institutes Board of War
520	Silla promulgates civil and penal code, establishes official clothing for officialdom
521	Silla offers tribute to Chinese Liang dynasty following Paekche embassy
522	Silla: Kaya king sends emissary requesting marriage alliance; Silla king sends the daughter of the *ich'an* (rank 2) Pijobu
525	Paekche constructs Tomb of King Muryŏng
527/528	Silla: Ich'adon martyred; Buddhism accepted as a state religion
529	Silla king Pŏphŭng prohibits the killing of living beings
531	Silla: *ich'an* Ch'ŏlbu is made senior grandee and entrusted with affairs of state

532	Silla: Kŭmgwan Kaya king Kim Kuhae surrenders his kingdom to Silla and is absorbed by Silla
535	Silla king Pŏphŭng begins work on first Buddhist complex, Hŭngnyun Monastery
536	Silla declares first reign-era title, 'Establishing Prime' (Kŏnwŏn)
538	Paekche moves capital to Sabi (present-day Puyŏ) and changes state designation to 'Southern Puyŏ' (Nam Puyŏ); establishes 22 central government offices
538/552	Paekche king dispatches monk Norisach'igye to introduce Buddhism to proto-Japanese Wa court
538	Silla king instructs officials receiving appointments to the prefectures to take their families
540–76	Silla king Chinhŭng establishes the *hwarang* ('flower boys')
545	Silla noble Kŏch'ilbu commanded to compile the *State History* (*Kuksa*)
546	Koguryŏ state affairs in chaos due to the succession struggle between Ch'ugun and Segun
551	Silla–Paekche alliance wrests Han river basin away from Koguryŏ
551	Silla: Koguryŏ monk Hyeryang takes refuge in Silla
551–76	Silla: Koguryŏ monk Hyeryang institutes Assembly of Eight Prohibitions (*p'algwanhoe*) and Convocation for the Recitation of the *Sūtra for Humane Kings* by One Hundred Eminent Monks (*paekkojwa kanghoe*)
552	Silla: Kaya musician Urŭk teaches Silla students how to play the *kayagŭm* (twelve-stringed Kaya zither), sing and dance

552	Koguryŏ: Wang Sanak redesigns the seven-stringed black zither (*qixuanqin*) and makes the *kŏmun'go* (six-stringed zither)
553	Silla seizes both the north and south sides of the Han river basin, dissolving the Silla–Paekche alliance
554	Paekche king Sŏng is killed in the Battle of Kwansan Fortress and suffers crushing defeat by Silla
555	Silla king Chinhŭng goes on royal inspection tour of Mount Pukhan and erects a commemorative stele
557	Koguryŏ revolt and execution of the noble Kan Churi, lord of Hwando Fortress
559–65	Silla monk Wŏn'gwang arrives in Chen to study Confucianism and Buddhism
562	Silla general Isabu conquers Tae Kaya
566	Silla begins construction of Hwangnyong Monastery
589	Reunification of China by Sui dynasty
590	Koguryŏ: Ondal dies in battle at Ach'a Fortress
598	Koguryŏ king leads an army of more than 10,000 Malgal troops and invades Liaoxi, but is driven back by the forces of Sui China
600	Koguryŏ: Yi Munjin compiles historical record called *New Collection* (*Sinjip*)
600	Paekche begins construction on Mirŭk Monastery
602	Silla noble youths Kwisan and Ch'uhang die in battle with Paekche after receiving the Five Secular Precepts (*sesok ogye*)
608/611	Silla monk Wŏn'gwang composes memorial for the Silla king requesting that Sui Chinese troops invade Koguryŏ; it is delivered to the Sui court

610	Koguryŏ monks Tamjing and Pŏpchŏng transmit the skills for making paper, Chinese ink and water mills to Japan; Tamjing makes wall paintings in the Golden Hall of Hōryūji
611	Paekche defeats Silla in the Battle of Kajam Fortress; Silla district magistrate Ch'andŏk dies heroically in battle
612	Koguryŏ: Sui makes first invasion attempt in first and second months; makes second invasion attempt on Koguryŏ in fifth to seventh months with a great force of 1,113,800; they besiege Koguryŏ's Yodong (Liaodong) Fortress; they advance as far as the Sal river, but they are defeated in a great rout by Koguryŏ general Ŭlchi Mundŏk
613	Koguryŏ: Sui makes third invasion attempt and fails
614	Koguryŏ: Sui makes fourth invasion attempt and fails
618	Chinese Tang dynasty replaces Sui dynasty
618	Silla district magistrate Ch'andŏk's son Hyeron dies in battle at Kajam Fortress
631	Koguryŏ begins work on a great wall (completed seventeen years later)
632	Silla queen Sŏndŏk ascends throne
641	Paekche king Ŭija ascends throne; known as the 'Zengzi of Haedong [Korea]'
642	Koguryŏ general Yŏn Kaesomun stages successful *coup d'état* and places King Pojang on throne
642	Paekche seizes forty Silla fortresses and storms Taeya Fortress; Silla noble Kim Ch'unch'u's son-in-law, castle lord Kim P'umsŏk, and his daughter die in the battle

642	Silla noble Kim Ch'unch'u enters Koguryŏ as diplomat to request troops against Paekche; he is detained in prison; he successfully uses the story of the turtle and the rabbit to escape imprisonment
645	Koguryŏ: Tang emperor Taizong invades; Koguryŏ victorious in Battle of Ansi Fortress
646	Silla completes building of nine-storey wooden pagoda at Hwangnyong Monastery
647	Silla general Kim Yusin suppresses revolt of senior grandee Pidam; Queen Chindŏk ascends throne
648	Silla noble Kim Ch'unch'u concludes an agreement with Tang emperor Taizong
649	Silla adopts Tang-style official dress
650	Silla starts using Tang reign era and offers tribute of 'Song of Great Peace' embroidered on silk
654	Silla: Kim Ch'unch'u, King T'aejong Muyŏl, ascends throne
660	Combined forces of Silla and Tang attack and conquer Paekche
661	Silla: death of King T'aejong; King Munmu ascends throne
663	Tang institutes the Jilin [Kyerim] area command in Silla and nominates King Munmu as its commander-in-chief
665	Tang institutes Xiongjin [Ungjin] area command in former Paekche territory; Paekche prince Puyŏ Yung returns to the peninsula as commander-in-chief
665	Koguryŏ: death of Yŏn Kaesomun
668	Combined forces of Silla and Tang attack and conquer Koguryŏ; Koguryŏ restoration movement begins
669	Tang institutes the Andong area command in former Koguryŏ territory; Silla begins attacks on Tang positions

670	Silla enfeoffs Ansŭng, a member of the Koguryŏ royal family, as king of Koguryŏ at Kŭmmajŏ
671	Silla monk Ŭisang returns to Silla with news of impending Tang naval invasion
673	Silla: death of general Kim Yusin
675	Silla: Battle of Maeso Fortress; defeat 200,000 Tang troops
676	Silla: Battle of Kibŏlp'o; Tang forces on peninsula make fighting retreat and evacuation from peninsula; Silla completes unification of Three Kingdoms; Ŭisang founds Pusŏk Monastery
681	Silla: passing of Silla king Munmu; King Sinmun ascends throne; Kim Hŭmdol rebellion fails
682	Silla establishes State Academy; Sinmun founds Kamŭn Monastery as votive temple for his father, Munmu
684	Silla: Koguryŏ remnant peoples foment an uprising at Kŭmmajŏ; government troops suppress the insurrection
686	Silla: passing of Buddhist exegete Wŏnhyo
687	Silla king Sinmun initiates system of granting office land, formalizes the nine prefectures and five minor capitals
689	Silla king Sinmun eliminates systems of stipend villages and establishes a graded system of annual grain grants
690	Tang empress Wu Zetian ascends the throne, declares Zhou dynasty
698	Parhae: Tae Choyŏng (King Ko) founds Parhae
702	Silla: passing of Buddhist monk Ŭisang, founder of Hwaŏm school
704	Silla: Kim Taemun, author of *Generations of the Hwarang* (*Hwarang segi*) and *Lives of Eminent Korean Monks* (*Kosŭng chŏn*), serves as commander-in-chief of Hansan prefecture

705	Tang: death of Empress Wu; restoration of the Tang imperial family
713	Parhae: Tang officially invests Tae Choyŏng as 'king of Parhae'
719	Parhae king Ko dies and King Mu ascends throne
721	Silla constructs great wall in Kangnŭng
722	Silla allocates farmland to adult males
727	Parhae pursues diplomatic relations with Japan; Silla monk Hyech'o returns to Tang from India and composes *Memoir of a Pilgrimage to the Five Regions of India* (*Wang och'ŏnch'ukkuk chŏn*)
733	Parhae engages in a naval military expedition, attacking Dengzhou on the Shandong peninsula; Tang and Silla form an alliance to attack Parhae
735	Silla: Tang formally recognizes Silla territory south of the Taedong river
737	Parhae king Mun ascends the throne
751–75	Silla noble Kim Taesŏng works on Pulguk Monastery and Sŏkkuram
755–63	Tang: An Lushan–Shi Siming rebellion in northern China
756	Parhae relocates its capital to Sanggyŏng ('upper capital'), Yongch'ŏnbu
757	Silla king Kyŏngdŏk reinstitutes stipend-land system and terminates office-land system and annual grain grants as means of paying officials
765	Silla monk Master Ch'ungdam composes native song (*hyangga*) 'Song of Pacifying the People' ('Anmin ka')
768	Silla revolt of the *ilgilch'an* (rank 7) Taegong and the *ach'an* (rank 6) Taeryŏm, also called the Revolt of the Ninety-Six *Kakkans*
770	Silla: rebellion of *taeach'an* (rank 5) Kim Yong
775	Silla: rebellion of *ach'an* (rank 6) Yŏmsang and Chŏngmun

780	Silla: rebellion of *ich'an* (rank 2) Kim Chijŏng; rebels lay siege to the palace and kill Silla king Hyegong; rebellion suppressed by senior grandee Kim Yangsang and the *ich'an* Kim Kyŏngsin; Kim Yangsang ascends throne as King Sŏndŏk
788	Silla king Wŏnsŏng institutes the curriculum of 'three degrees of reading books' (*toksŏ samp'um*)
802	Silla: founding of Haein Monastery
822	Silla: rebellion of Kim Hŏnch'ang
828	Silla: Chang Pogo establishes Ch'ŏnghae garrison on Wan Island
860	Silla: *hwarang* Kim Ŭngnyŏm marries elder daughter of King Hŏnan and becomes heir apparent
874	Silla scholar Ch'oe Ch'iwŏn passes the civil service exam in Tang
875–84	Tang: Huang Chao rebellion in China
879	Silla scholar Ch'oe Ch'iwŏn earns fame in Tang by composing the 'Declaration Denouncing Huang Chao' ('T'o Hwang So kyŏngmun')
886	Ch'oe Ch'iwŏn returns to Silla
887	Silla queen Chinsŏng ascends throne; filial daughter Chiŭn recognized by government
888	Silla senior grandee Kim Wihong and Buddhist monk Taegu collect extant native songs and compile the *Collection from the Three Reign Periods* (*Samdaemok*); Wang Kŏin cast into prison for anti-government behaviour
889	Silla: Wŏnjong and Aeno lead commoners in rebellion in Sabŏlchu (Sangju)
891	Under direction of bandit leader Yanggil, Kungye attacks villages loyal to Silla in northern prefectures
892	Kyŏn Hwŏn leads uprising in Silla's southwestern prefectures

894	Ch'oe Ch'iwŏn presents ten recommendations to Silla court; Kungye becomes independent from Yanggil
895	Kungye calls himself 'Dynasty-Founding Lord' (*kaegukkun*), establishes 'Later Koguryŏ' and makes subordinate Wang Kŏn the grand protector of Ch'ŏrwŏn commandery
896	Red Trouser rebellion in southwest Silla
899	Bandit leader Yanggil attacks Kungye, but suffers crushing defeat
900	Kyŏn Hwŏn calls himself 'king' and establishes 'Later Paekche' in Wansanju; several of Yanggil's commanders switch allegiance to Kungye
901	Kungye assumes title of 'king'; Kyŏn Hwŏn attacks Silla's Taeya Fortress
904	Kungye establishes government offices following Silla pattern and names country Majin
907	Tang dynasty ends
911	Kungye renames his state Majin as T'aebong
916	Khitans (Qidan) found Liao dynasty (916–1125) in northern China
918	Wang Kŏn removes Kungye in coup and renames T'aebong as Koryŏ
925	Parhae subjects seek refuge in Koryŏ
926	Parhae conquered by Khitans
927	Silla capital sacked by Later Paekche; Kyŏn Hwŏn kills Silla king and places King Kyŏngsun on Silla throne
935	Silla king Kyŏngsun surrenders to Wang Kŏn; Silla capital is renamed Kyŏngju
936	Later Paekche surrenders to Wang Kŏn; Korean peninsula united under Koryŏ state

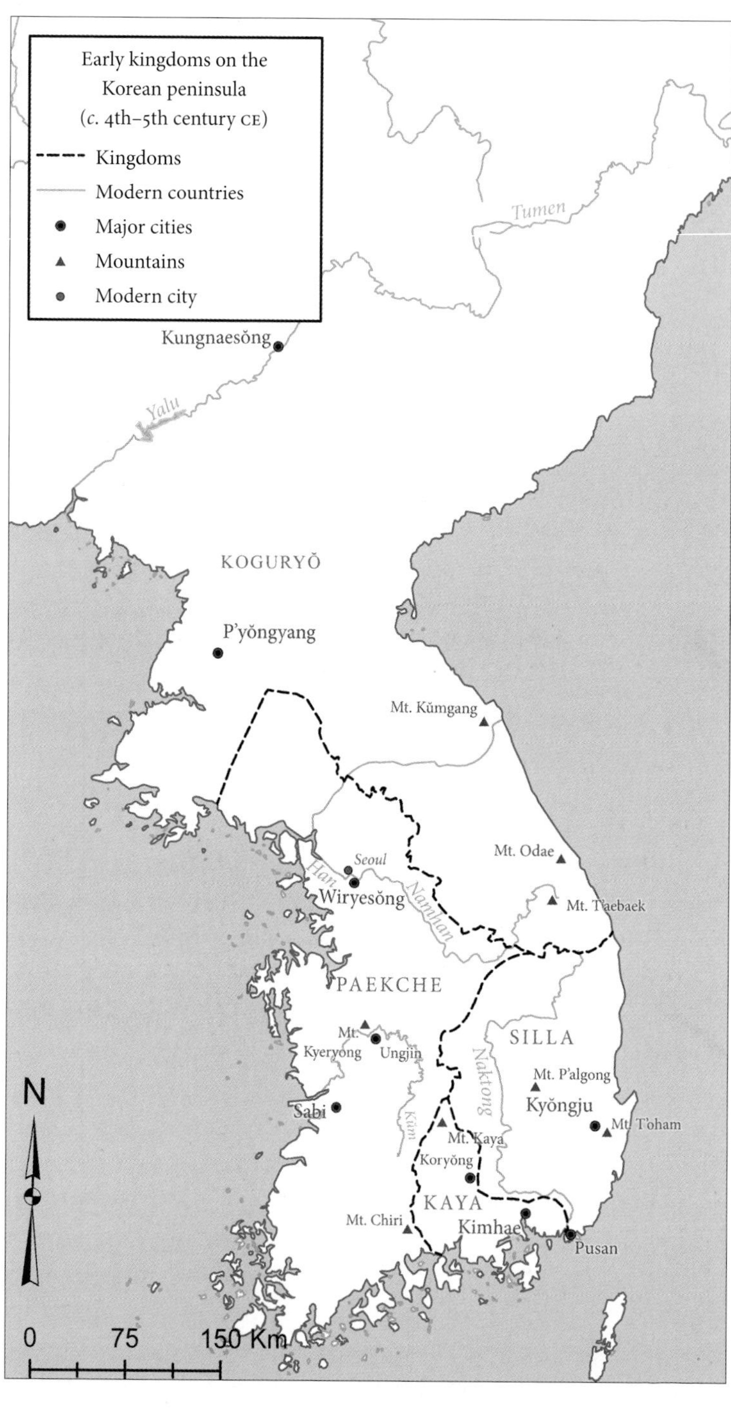
Early kingdoms on the Korean peninsula (c. 4th–5th century CE)
Kingdoms
Modern countries
Major cities
Mountains
Modern city
Tumen
Kungnaesŏng
Yalu
KOGURYŎ
P'yŏngyang
Mt. Kŭmgang
Mt. Odae
Seoul
Han
Wiryesŏng
Namhan
Mt. T'aebaek
PAEKCHE
SILLA
Mt. Kyeryong
Ungjin
Naktong
Mt. P'algong
Sabi
Kŭm
Kyŏngju
Mt. T'oham
Mt. Kaya
Koryŏng
KAYA
Mt. Chiri
Kimhae
Pusan
N
0
75
150 Km

INTRODUCTION

In recent years, people throughout the world have become exposed to the stories and society of Korea's lost early civilization through such engaging historical dramas as *Jumong* (2006–7), *Queen Seondeok* (2009) and *Hwarang: The Poet Warrior Youth* (2016–17). Besides enamouring outsiders with fascinating and captivating aspects of ancient Korean history, these dramas breathe life – as well as a good measure of spectacular imagination – into some of the most compelling narratives that have shaped Koreans' views of themselves and the earliest descriptions of their culture. Korean antiquity is commonly referred to as the 'Three Kingdoms period'.

The Three Kingdoms period (traditionally dated from 57 BCE to 935 CE) of Korean history was not only formative in terms of the creation and crafting of Korean identity and cultural patterns, but a period of social, political, religious and intellectual dynamism. During this age, the peoples of the Korean peninsula were divided regionally into several competing states that, at least in the eyes of outside Chinese observers, shared some similar characteristics in language and culture. The three primary kingdoms alluded to are the militaristic Koguryŏ (traditionally dated from 37 BCE to 668 CE) in the north, the culturally sophisticated Paekche (traditionally 18 BCE to 660 CE) in the southwest, and the highly socially stratified Silla (traditionally 57 BCE to 935 CE) in the southeast. However, a fourth confederation of states unified with the name Kaya (traditionally 42 to 562 CE) flourished in south central Korea in the Naktong river basin from the first century CE, and was assimilated into both Silla and Paekche in the mid-sixth century. Similar to how Christianity served as a conduit to introduce advanced Roman culture to the fledgling Germanic states of medieval Europe and strengthen notions of kingship, Buddhism was the vehicle by which refined aspects of Chinese culture and technology and Confucian statecraft entered and transformed Northeast Asia.

Although the state of Silla was the most conservative and culturally the least polished of the early Korean states, after the adoption of Buddhism it became increasingly dynamic and socially stratified. Ultimately, by means of a complex alliance with Tang China (618–907), Paekche and Koguryŏ were conquered in 660 and 668 respectively. After successfully expelling Tang forces from their expanded dominion in the 670s, Silla gained control of the peninsula south of the Taedong river. In the old Koguryŏ domain in Manchuria, however, the Parhae state (698–926) arose, claiming to be the legitimate successor to Koguryŏ. A hybrid state comprising remnant peoples of Koguryŏ and Malgal tribespeople, Parhae thrived in the eighth and ninth centuries. The latter half of the Three Kingdoms period has conventionally been referred to as the 'Unified Silla' period (668–935), following Japanese and Korean scholarship, but beginning in the latter half of the twentieth century some Korean scholars returned to the Koryŏ-period historian Kim Pusik's (1075–1151) characterization of middle (654–780) and late (780–935) Silla periods while others advanced the idea of a Korean Northern and Southern Dynasties period, with a Greater Silla in the south and Parhae in the north. I will use the term 'Greater Silla' for simplicity's sake in this book. With the decline of Silla in the late ninth century, kingdoms of the Later Koguryŏ and Later Paekche re-emerged, such that this age closes with a Later Three Kingdoms period in the tenth century. Thus 'Three Kingdoms' serves as a useful general term for a roughly thousand-year period of early Korean history.

The two main literary sources for the study of Korea's Three Kingdoms period are the *History of the Three Kingdoms* (*Samguk sagi*) and *Memorabilia of the Three Kingdoms* (*Samguk yusa*). The former was compiled by a team under the direction of the scholar-official Kim Pusik between 1142 and 1145, which was officially presented at court in 1146, and follows the structure established by the Chinese historians Sima Tan (*c.* 180–110 BCE) and Sima Qian's (146–86 BCE) *Records of the Grand Historian* (*Shiji*). Like other Chinese dynastic histories that also follow the pattern set by this text, Buddhist themes are not treated in detail and are overlooked and disregarded in many respects. In addition, Kim Pusik drew heavily on Chinese historical literature to supplement the dearth of native Korean material. Historical anachronisms, improbably long reign dates in early king lists and other dating problems are evident in a close reading of the text. Notwithstanding these shortcomings, *History of the Three Kingdoms* preserves important information on government offices and systems, society and geography, as well as crucial information about the Silla royal family's use of Buddhist symbolism to provide legitimacy vis-à-vis the state's formidable hereditary nobility.

Memorabilia of the Three Kingdoms was compiled initially by the Buddhist monk Iryŏn (1206–1289), probably started in his later years (*c.* 1285) during or after the destructive Mongol conquest and subjugation of Korea in the mid-thirteenth century. The collection was further added to by his disciple Mugŭk (Hon'gu, 1250–1322) and also by later unknown contributors. It was likely first published in 1394, but the received edition of the text was published in 1512. The work is a melange of legends of historical personages, places and events, and of short stories, local narratives, Buddhist-oriented origin accounts, strange tales, poetry, songs and so forth. Although many scholars educated in Korea do not question its validity, researchers trained outside Korea are predictably sceptical of the value of *Memorabilia of the Three Kingdoms*, not only because of its late date but because of the fantastic nature of much of its subject-matter and anachronisms. The text was first compiled during the transition from the mid- to late Koryŏ period, but many of the stories it includes originate from accounts found in earlier documents, biographies, inscriptions on steles, images, gazetteers and collections of wonder tales. Much of the material in the book provides an illustration of the traditions and local discourse of the Silla kingdom. Although the editorial hand of Iryŏn and others is obvious and unavoidable, *Memorabilia of the Three Kingdoms* preserves much of the original language of its sources as far as such sources can be checked. For all its shortcomings, it is an important source for how Koreans of later periods and today imagine the splendour of the Three Kingdoms period.

Fortunately, these literary materials are complemented with a comparatively abundant corpus of inscriptions, primarily from the Silla kingdom, as well as Buddhist commentarial literature, and mentions of the Three Kingdoms in contemporary Chinese and Japanese historiographical literature.

This book presents a systematic overview of the dynamic history and culture of the Three Kingdoms period by first treating the legendary accounts of the founding of the ancient kingdoms and then placing the origins of these states in their historical contexts. It then describes the rise and development of the kingdoms of Koguryŏ, Paekche, Kaya and Silla. The coverage of the early Three Kingdoms period closes with a brief examination of the role of religion in ancient Korean states, the adoption of Confucianism, Daoism and Buddhism from China and the adaptation of these teachings to Korean culture. The narrative will then consider Greater Silla and Parhae and the flourishing of Buddhism and Confucianism in Greater Silla. The book concludes with a brief treatment of the Later Three Kingdoms period.

ONE

Legends and Origins of Korea's Three Kingdoms

Koreans usually trace their history back to an ancient polity conventionally called 'Old Chosŏn' – to distinguish it from the later Chosŏn dynasty (1392–1910) – that existed in the basins of the Liao and Taedong rivers, centred in the area of present-day P'yŏngyang. A bronze culture of Scytho-Siberian origin and Chinese iron culture merged in Old Chosŏn, and the people developed uses for these technologies that would eventually differentiate Koreans from other Northeast Asian peoples, such as *ondol* heating installations – an arrangement of flues under the floor. Later legends, which are beyond the purposes of this chapter, allege the founding of Old Chosŏn in remote antiquity by a demigod named Tan'gun in 2333 BCE or by an émigré from Shang China named Kija (Jizi in Chinese) in 1122 BCE. Old Chosŏn, which most likely emerged in the fifth century BCE, declined with the rise of the powerful Chinese Yan state, which invaded the Liaodong peninsula at the end of the fourth century BCE. After the fall of Yan to the Han dynasty in 206 BCE, refugees from Yan appear to have filtered into Old Chosŏn, which was then ruled by a certain King Chun. Among these was a certain Wei Man (Wiman in Korean), who gained a band of followers and drove the king of Old Chosŏn from his throne. Wiman (r. *c.* 194–180 BCE) and his successors ruled what Korean historians have called Wiman Chosŏn until Han emperor Wu (r. 141–87 BCE) conquered it in 108 BCE and established four commanderies to collect tribute and regulate the tribal peoples living there. Meanwhile, the ousted King Chun is said to have escaped southward to the state of Chin and established himself as the 'Han king'.

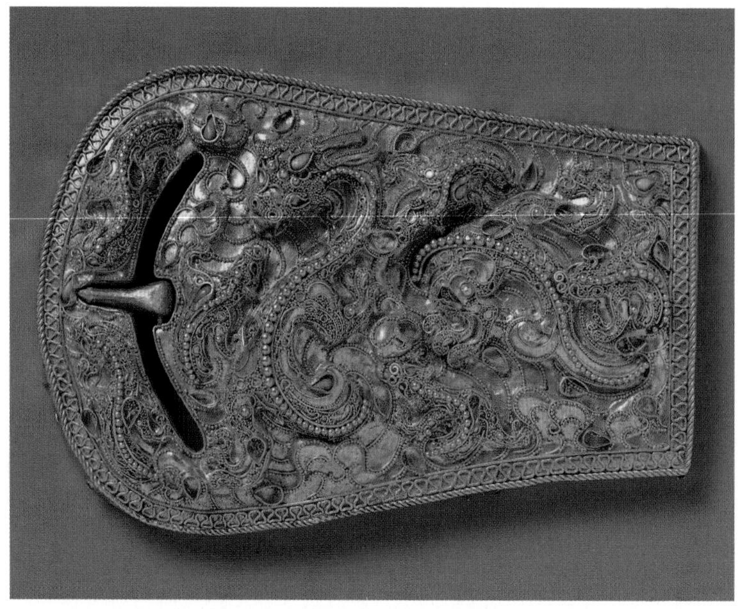

Sŏgamni gold buckle of P'yŏngyang, Lelang commandery, mid-1st century CE, gold.

The Chin polity, located south of the Han river near present-day Seoul, is first mentioned in connection with an event of the second century BCE, when Wiman Chosŏn controlled the Taedong river basin. Representatives of Chin attempted to open up direct communication with Han China, which suggests a desire on the part of this early Korean polity to reap the benefits of Chinese metal culture. Scholars opine that refugees from Old Chosŏn, many of whom were skilled in metalworking technologies, moved southward and that these people caused a transformation, enabling the development of the Three Han states (Samhan) that will be treated below.

Many tribal peoples figure in the origins of the Korean people. Far to the north of Old Chosŏn, the Puyŏ polity flourished in the centre of present-day Jilin province between the northward-flowing Songhua river and the Dongliao river. The tribal names Ye and Maek, also called Yemaek and sometimes just Maek, are general terms referring to the peoples who inhabited the Liaodong region and eastward, including the northern part of the Korean peninsula. The Okchŏ were another tribal people active before and after the third century CE who were located on the coast that stretches to the northeast of present-day Hamhŭng.

The role of the four Han Chinese commanderies in the development of the early Korean states is a contentious topic in modern Korea. Not only are the history and archaeology of the Chinese presence on the Korean peninsula stimulating and challenging by themselves, but the study of the Han commanderies is doubly perplexing primarily due to problematical assertions made by nationalistic scholars and pseudo-historians. Because this topic is also beyond the scope of this short book, the basics may be outlined as follows: after Han emperor Wu conquered Wiman Chosŏn, he established four commanderies in 108 and 107 BCE to facilitate and regulate relations with and between the various proto-Korean tribal peoples both in Manchuria and in the northern part of the Korean peninsula. The most important and long-lasting of these

Lelang *bi* disc, Lelang commandery, mid-1st century CE, jade.

was the Lelang commandery centred at present-day P'yŏngyang. The Zhenfan and Lintun commanderies were established to control, respectively, the Chinbŏn and Ye peoples of the east coast. These were abolished in 82 BCE and their subordinate districts given to Lelang. The Xuantu commandery was originally established to regulate the Okchŏ, but it was invaded by local indigenous groups. It was re-established westward in Yongling in 75 BCE, and the Chinese attempted to use it to control relations between Puyŏ, Koguryŏ and other groups. Other factors contributing to alterations of these kinds include changes in Chinese frontier policy and variations in the ethnic composition of the commanderies. The Daifang commandery, instituted in the early third century in the present-day Hwanghae provinces in North Korea, was essentially in the same place as the original Zhenfan commandery. It was intended to regulate the populations, both indigenous and Chinese, that were migrating southward towards the Han states because the Lelang commandery was struggling to maintain control over its people.

This chapter will briefly introduce the foundation myths of the early Korean states, several of which emerged and evolved in this complex milieu of the movement and assimilation of peoples in northern China, Manchuria and the Korean peninsula.

Lelang bear-shaped table legs, Lelang commandery, mid-1st century CE, gilt bronze.

The Puyŏ Foundation Myth

Although the ancient Manchurian state of Puyŏ (?–346 CE) is not, strictly speaking, one of the Three Kingdoms of early Korea, we must begin with a discussion of Puyŏ's foundation myth to understand the founding legends of Koguryŏ and Paekche. The Puyŏ story, which likely derived from the testimony of the Puyŏ people themselves, is recorded in *Doctrines Evaluated* (*Lunheng*), a late first-century collection of philosophical essays composed by the Chinese thinker Wang Chong (27–*c.* 100 CE):

> A waiting maid of the king of T'angni (Tuoli in Chinese), a barbarian state in the north, became pregnant, and the king wanted to kill her. The girl said that a spirit as big as a hen's egg had come down from Heaven, and that it was by this that she had conceived. [When] she later gave birth to the child, it was cast into a pigsty, but the pigs breathed upon it with their breath and it did not die; so, it was taken away and laid in a stable to be trodden to death, but the horses also breathed upon it with their breath and it did not die. Then, the king, suspecting it might be Heaven's son, let the mother take it back and had [the boy] brought up as a slave … giving him the name Tongmyŏng (Dongming in Chinese), and ordering him to look after the cattle and horses. Tongmyŏng became such a fine archer that the king feared that he might seize the kingdom and wanted to kill him. Tongmyŏng fled south until he came to the river Ŏmho (Yanhu in Chinese), where he struck the water with his bow. Fishes and mud-turtles floated up and made a bridge, but as soon as Tongmyŏng had got across the fish and mud-turtles dispersed, so that the soldiers pursuing [Tongmyŏng] could not cross over. Thereupon, Tongmyŏng founded a capital and became king of Puyŏ (Fuyu in Chinese). This accounts for the existence of Puyŏ as a barbarian kingdom in the north.[1]

The tale describes how the young Tongmyŏng, who is the offspring of divine and miraculous conception, flees southward from the state of T'angni and founds Puyŏ. Strange or unorthodox birth stories like Tongmyŏng's were not uncommon among peoples in Northeast Asia. The *Book of Songs* reports that Lord Millet, the ancestor of the Zhou people who conquered the ancient Shang dynasty in China, was conceived when his mother trod on the big toe of a deity's footprint. The *Monograph on the Three Kingdoms* (*Sanguo zhi*) and *History of the Later Han Dynasty* (*Hou Han shu*) report that Tanshihuai, a second-century Xianbei ruler, was born after his mother accidentally swallowed a hailstone that had fallen from heaven.

Koguryŏ

The tale of Tongmyŏng is particularly relevant for the case of Koguryŏ because it reappears in nearly identical form as the foundation myth of the Koguryŏ state. The oldest recorded version of the story was carved in about 414 on the 'Inscription on the Stele Erected in Honour of King Kwanggaet'o' ('Kwanggaet'o wangnŭng pi'):

> Of old, when our First Ancestor King Ch'umo laid the foundation of our state, he came forth from Northern Puyŏ as the offspring of the Celestial Thearch (*ch'ŏnje*). His mother, the daughter of the Earl of the River (Habaek), gave birth to him by cracking an egg and bringing her child forth from it. Endowed with heavenly virtue, King Ch'umo [accepted his mother's command and] made a royal tour to the south. His route went by way of Puyŏ's Great Ŏmni River. Gazing over the ford, the king said, 'I am King Ch'umo, offspring of August Heaven (*hwangch'ŏn*) and of the daughter of the Earl of the River. Weave together the bulrushes for me so that the turtles will float to the surface.' And no sooner had he spoken than [the God of the River] wove the bulrushes so that the turtles floated to the surface, whereupon he crossed the river. Upon the mountain fortress west of Cholbon in Piryu Valley he established his capital, wherein his family would long enjoy the hereditary position. Accordingly, he [ritually] summoned

Stele erected in honour of King Kwanggaet'o, Ji'an, China, *c*. 414.

the Yellow Dragon to come down and 'meet the king'. The king was on the hill east of Cholbon, and the Yellow Dragon took him on its back and ascended to Heaven. He left a testamentary command to his heir apparent, King Yuryu, that he should conduct his government in accordance with the Way. Great King Churyu succeeded to the rule, and the throne was

Ornamental dagger sheath, Silla, 5th century.

> handed on, [eventually] to the seventeenth in succession, Kukkangsang Kwanggaet'o Kyŏngp'yŏng Anho T'aewang.[2]

Other versions of the tradition of Koguryŏ's first ancestor are found in Chinese dynastic histories. The oldest among these is the version found in the *History of the Northern Wei* (*Wei shu*), which was compiled between 551 and 554. In the Chinese versions he is called Chumong, which is said to mean 'shoots arrows well'. When his mother gave birth to an egg, the Puyŏ king gave it to a dog to eat, but the dog did not eat it. He then gave it to a pig, but the pig did not eat it. He then cast it out onto the road, but cows and horses would not trample it. After a bird wrapped its wings protectively around it when it was thrown onto a field, the king relented and returned it to his mother. Because of his superior martial skills, the people of Puyŏ sought to kill him; so, following his mother's advice, Chumong fled Puyŏ with a few close friends. When the pursuit by Puyŏ subjects became intense, he miraculously crossed a river on the backs of fish and turtles. Eventually he settled at Hŭlsŭnggolsŏng, which became the first Koguryŏ capital.

The narrative in the *History of the Three Kingdoms* is reportedly a summary of the 'Lay of King Tongmyŏng' ('Tongmyŏng Wang p'yŏn') in the now-lost *Old History of the Three Kingdoms* (*Ku Samguksa*). The Koryŏ scholar Yi Kyubo (1168–1241) also crafted a detailed verse summary of the 'Lay of King Tongmyŏng'. These show an even more direct connection with the Puyŏ legend because here the founder of Koguryŏ is unabashedly named 'The Sage King Tongmyŏng'. The *History of the Three Kingdoms* version fleshes out the story with a greatly expanded narrative and emphasizes places where this fully developed story differs from the version found in the *History of the Northern Wei*. In this version, the story begins by describing the miraculous birth of the golden boy Kŭmwa (Golden Frog) in Puyŏ and his becoming heir apparent because the king has no offspring. The old Puyŏ king is persuaded by his grand councillor to move the Puyŏ capital to 'Eastern Puyŏ', and the old, original Puyŏ capital is occupied by Haemosu, the son of the Heavenly Emperor. Kŭmwa ascended the throne when Haemosu died and discovered a beautiful young girl south of Mount T'aebaek named Yuhwa (Willow Flower), the daughter of the Earl of the River. Yuhwa described how she met the lad Haemosu and gave herself to him. Kŭmwa brought Yuhwa back to his capital and shut her up in a room. After she gave birth to a large egg, the king had it thrown to dogs, pigs and birds, as in the earlier version reviewed above. When the king's men had given up breaking the egg, the king returned it to Yuhwa. Eventually a fine baby boy was born. He had the appearance of a hero and was an outstanding archer, so they named him Chumong.

Kŭmwa had seven sons who often played with Chumong, but none of them were his match. Not only was Chumong the best archer, but his knowledge of horses surpassed all others as well. Kŭmwa's sons and ministers attempted to murder Chumong several times, because they considered him a threat, so Chumong and his friends decided to leave Puyŏ and travel to a distant land. Travelling southward, Chumong wanted to cross the Ŏmch'e river and declared himself the offspring of the Heavenly Emperor and the Earl of the River. In response, the fishes and turtles formed a bridge for him to cross. Chumong encountered people on the way, gave them surnames and declared that he planned to found a new kingdom. He eventually settled on the banks of the Piryu river (Cholbon Puyŏ), called his kingdom Koguryŏ and adopted Ko ('high', 'lofty') as his surname. This is said to have happened in 37 BCE. Koguryŏ bordered on the lands of the Malgal tribal peoples (Mohe in Chinese), and Chumong subjugated them to him. The legend ends with Chumong competing against Songyang, the king of Piryu, in archery, and handily defeating him due to his prowess, thus becoming the sole ruler of the area. The 'Lay of King Tongmyŏng' ends with Chumong mounting a dragon and ascending to heaven at the time of his death.

Paekche

The Paekche foundation myth builds upon the Koguryŏ foundation myth, drawing legitimacy from either real or imagined connections with Puyŏ.

Patterned tile with animal design, excavated from Oeri, Puyŏ, Paekche, 6th century.

As preserved in the *History of the Three Kingdoms*, the story of the founding of Paekche asserts a close connection with both Puyŏ and Koguryŏ. Onjo, the founder of Paekche, is said to be a son of Ch'umo or Chumong, the founder of Koguryŏ, who left because his opportunity to inherit his father's position was upset by the arrival of an elder brother who became his father's heir apparent:

> The founder of Paekche was King Onjo. His father was Ch'umo, sometimes called Chumong. Fleeing from Northern Puyŏ to escape troubles, Chumong arrived in Cholbon Puyŏ. The [Cholbon] Puyŏ king did not have an heir, but he had three daughters. Seeing Chumong, the king realized that he was an extraordinary person and offered his second daughter in marriage. Soon thereafter, the [Cholbon] Puyŏ king died and

> Chumong succeeded him to the throne. Chumong's wife gave birth to two sons: the elder was named Piryu and the younger Onjo. (It is also said that when Chumong reached Cholbon, he married a woman of Wŏlgun, who gave birth to two sons.) At a later time, a son whom Chumong had fathered previously while he was living in Northern Puyŏ was designated as heir apparent. Piryu and Onjo, afraid that they would be mistreated by the crown prince, thereupon departed and travelled south with ten retainers, including Ogan and Maryŏ, and a great number of followers among common people. They subsequently arrived at Mount Han, climbed Pua Peak, and looked over the surrounding terrain for a site suitable for settlement. Piryu desired to dwell by the seashore, but the ten retainers remonstrated with him, 'Consider the land there below us to the south of the Han River. In the north it is bounded by the river, to the east it is nestled against high peaks, to the south it overlooks fertile wetlands, and to the west it is protected by the great sea. This area of natural barriers and favourable land possesses virtues difficult to find. Would it not be most appropriate to make our settlement here?' Piryu did not heed their advice. Dividing the people who had followed them, he removed to Mich'uhol and settled there. Onjo's capital was Wiryesŏng to the south of the river. Because the ten retainers had assisted him, he named his country Sipche ('The Ten Auxiliaries'). These events occurred in the third year of the Hongjia reign period (18 BCE) of Emperor Cheng (r. 32–6 BCE) of the Former Han dynasty.[3]

Although the legend tracing Paekche's founding through Onjo eventually became the most popular, an interlinear note in the *History of the Three Kingdoms* also preserves a variant version of Paekche's founding through Piryu:

> The dynastic founder was King Piryu and his father was Ut'ae, the grandson by a concubine of King Hae Puru of Northern Puyŏ. His mother was Sosŏno, the daughter of Yŏn T'abal, a native of Cholbon [Puyŏ]. After giving herself to Ut'ae, she

gave birth to two sons, the elder Piryu and the younger Onjo. Once Ut'ae died, his widow [Sosŏno] dwelt in Cholbon [with her two sons]. Later, when Chumong was no longer tolerated in [Northern] Puyŏ – which dates to the spring, the second month of the second year of the Jianzhao reign period of the Former Han (37 BCE) – he fled south to Cholbon, where he established his capital and called his state Koguryŏ. [Chumong] took Sosŏno as his wife and made her his consort. Because she provided valuable assistance in the founding of his state, Chumong rewarded her with special favour and treated Piryu and Onjo as if they were his own children. At a later time, when Yuryu, Chumong's son who had been born earlier to a woman of the Ye clan while he was still living in [Northern] Puyŏ, came to his father's court, the king invested him as heir apparent in order to settle the succession to the throne.

Consequently, [when Yuryu succeeded to the throne in 19 BCE], Piryu reasoned with his younger brother, Onjo, 'Formerly, when the Great King [Chumong] left [Northern] Puyŏ to avoid particular troubles there and fled to take refuge in this land, our mother expended her family's resources in aiding him to establish his rule. She truly exerted herself assiduously on his behalf! Now that the Great King has departed from this world and the state is under the control of Yuryu, if we and our followers were to remain here, it would be as difficult to endure as being afflicted with warts! Would we not better serve our mother by wandering south, taking possession of suitable land, and there establishing our own freestanding state?' Subsequently, he and his brother led their partisans forth and, after crossing the P'ae and Tae Rivers, they arrived at Mich'uhol, where they decided to dwell.

[By contrast,] the *History of the Northern Dynasties* (*Beishi*) and the *History of the Sui* (*Sui shu*) assert the following: 'Among the descendants of Tongmyŏng was Kut'ae, a man unswerving in his humaneness and trustworthiness. When he initially established his state in the former territory of the Daifang commandery, the governor of the Han commandery at Liaodong, Gongsun Du, presented Kut'ae with his daughter in marriage.

> Subsequently, Paekche became a powerful state among the "Eastern Barbarians".[4]

In the Koguryŏ story, Piryu is the name of a valley and a kingdom. In the Paekche story, it has morphed into the name of the founder king. The Chinese versions of Paekche's founding, however, are linked to the time when the Gongsun warlords ruled Liaodong (*c.* 189–238), as Gongsun Du (*c.* 150–204) is a known historical figure.

Kim Suro and the Founding of Kaya

The tale of Kim Suro (traditionally 42–199 CE) and the founding of Kŭmgwan Kaya, as preserved in *Memorabilia of the Three Kingdoms*, was initially recorded by a literatus, the prefect of Kŭmgwan, present-day Kimhae in South Kyŏngsang province, sometime between 1075 and 1084. According to this account, before the territory that would become Kaya even had a name, nine chiefs led the 75,000 people living in this region in gathering food in the mountains, digging wells for drinking water and cultivating fields for food.

On the day of the bathing purification rites in the third month of the eighteenth year of the Jianwu reign period (42 CE) in the reign of Shizu, Emperor Guangwu of the Later Han (r. 5 BCE–57 CE), there was a strange sound, as of someone calling, on a peak called Turtle Back (Kuji), located to the north of where they lived. After several hundred people had gathered, including the nine chiefs, the disembodied voice wanted to know where it was. The chiefs responded that it was at Turtle Back Peak. The voice then went on to declare,

> The Heavenly Emperor has instructed me to come to this place to create a new country and become its leader. For this reason, I have descended here. Dig on the ground at the peak of the mountain singing the verse, 'Turtle, Turtle, push out your head; if you do not, we shall cook and eat you.' If you sing and dance like this, you will have a great king and great joy.

Following this command, the nine chiefs sang and danced joyfully. They saw a purple rope hanging down from the sky, reaching the ground. A golden bowl wrapped in a red cloth was attached to the end of the rope. Upon opening it, the chiefs found six golden eggs, which were as round as the sun. The eggs were taken to one of the chief's homes, and after twelve days the eggs transformed into six infant boys. The six boys grew to a height of nine feet and matured after a mere ten days. The boy who appeared first was named Suro, and his country was called Great Karak or Kaya, which was one of the six Kaya states.

On the 27th day of the seventh month of *musin*, the 24th year of the Jianwu reign period (5 August 48 CE), the nine chiefs and other members of the court encouraged the king to take a young woman as queen. Suro demurred and said that because heaven had made him king, it would also provide a suitable queen. Suro sent the chief of a subordinate polity on a lightly laden ship to Mangsan Island, with a fine horse. The king told him to wait there. A ship suddenly appeared bearing the queen of a faraway country and members of her entourage. She acquiesced to the invitation to dock her boat, and Suro was overjoyed at the news of her arrival.

Later, when the king and queen were alone in the royal bedchamber, the queen gently said to the king,

> I am a princess from Ayut'a [Ayodhyā]. My family name is Hŏ and my personal name is Hwangok. I am sixteen years old. In the fifth month of this year, when I was still in my home country, my royal parents said to me, 'Last night in a dream we both saw the Heavenly Emperor, who said to us, "A man called Suro is the founder king of the state of Karak and was sent by Heaven to govern. He is indeed sacred and divine. In governing the new country, however, he has to be matched with an appropriate spouse. You should send your daughter to be his wife." When the Heavenly Emperor finished speaking, he ascended to heaven. After this dream, the words of the Heavenly Emperor continued to ring in our ears. You must quickly depart from here and go to Karak.' Thus, I have set to sea, searching for

> steamed dates and heavenly peaches, and now I have come to Your Majesty, who has a beautiful appearance.

The king replied, 'I have foreseen, since I was born, that a princess would come from a distant land. Although my officials requested that I marry a queen, I did not heed them. Now that you, a virtuous princess, have come to me on your own, I am indeed extremely fortunate.' Suro and his queen ruled the country like his own household, and he loved the people like his own children.

The founding story of the Kŭmgwan Kaya polity (traditional dates 42–532) highlights the importance of chiefs and tribal federations. Chiefs also play a role in the late foundation story of Silla. The *History of the Three Kingdoms* and the *Memorabilia of the Three Kingdoms* describe how the leaders of Sŏrabŏl's six regions met together and unanimously accepted a golden boy born from an egg – like Chumong – to be king of Silla.

The Evolution of Silla Foundation Stories

The *History of the Three Kingdoms* asserts that Silla's founding ancestor was discovered by a village chief named Lord Sobŏl who, looking at the foot of Mount Yang, saw a horse kneeling between two trees near the well of Najŏng. When the chief drew closer, he found no horse but a large egg. Splitting open the egg he discovered a boy whom the chiefs surnamed Pak, because the egg looked like a gourd, and who was named Hyŏkkŏse. Hyŏkkŏse was given the title *kŏsŏgan* ('king' or 'great khan') and ascended the throne in 57 BCE, being chosen to rule by the chiefs of the six regions of Sŏrabŏl, present-day Kyŏngju in North Kyŏngsang province. The

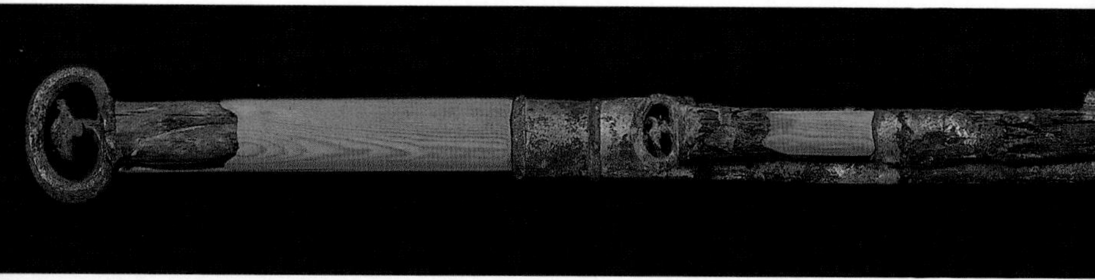

Silla throne would reportedly rotate among three descent groups – Pak, Sŏk and Kim – before settling firmly with the Kim clan in the mid-fourth century. *Memorabilia of the Three Kingdoms* preserves a relatively detailed account of the miraculous birth of this beautiful and bright boy from a large red egg that appeared after a flash of lightning, at the end of a rainbow near the sacred well Najŏng, and heralded by a kneeling white horse.

The problem with the story of Hyŏkkŏse, however, is that it was unknown in Silla times and was likely crafted in the early Koryŏ period. Archaeological and textual evidence from early Chinese dynastic histories indicates a date no earlier than the beginning of the fourth century CE for the emergence of Silla from the group of minor Chinhan polities. Silla epigraphy from the mid-sixth century – the time when Silla kings adopted the Kim surname – refers to an otherwise undefined 'Grand Ancestor' (*t'aejo*) as its founder. In addition, Chinese official histories compiled in the first half of the seventh century, such as the *History of the Liang Dynasty* and the *History of the Sui Dynasty*, generally agree that Silla was a state that formed around various immigrant peoples who were originally ruled by a king from Mahan. Silla epigraphy from the late seventh century to the early ninth refers to an obscure figure named Sŏnghan as the founding king of Silla, and the funerary stele of King Munmu (r. 661–81) plainly states that Sŏnghan was Munmu's fifteenth-generation ancestor. Munmu's stele also asserts that the Silla royal family are descendants of Du-hou (Marquis Du), a Xiongnu prince named Jin Midi (sometimes written Jin Ridi; Kim Ilche in Korean) who was loyal to the Han dynasty during the age of the great Han–Xiongnu war in the second century BCE. The inscription's declaration that the Silla royal family descended from

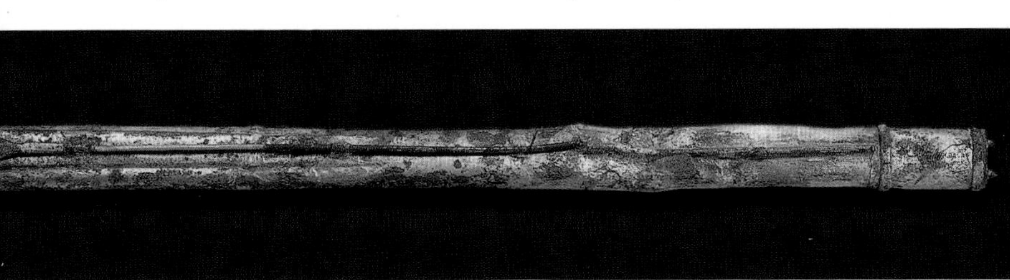

Sword with ring pommel, Kyŏngju, 6th century CE.

Gilt-bronze shoes, Silla, 5th century.

this Xiongnu noble was likely included for rhetorical and political purposes because Silla's relations with Tang China were strained due to their disagreement over supervision of the jointly conquered Paekche and Koguryŏ lands after the peninsular unification wars (*c.* 660–76).

The sixth-century Silla monarch Pŏphŭng (r. 514–40) probably emerged as a viable founding king during the eighth century, when the Silla royalty constructed Chinese-style ancestral temples following instructions set forth in the *Book of Rites*. This is because, during Pŏphŭng's reign, Buddhism was adopted as a state religion in about 527 and the Kŭmgwan Kaya state was absorbed into Silla in 532. By the reign of King Hyegong (765–80), King Mich'u (traditionally r. 262–84) was likely created as a double of Pŏphŭng, in order to push the origins of Silla back several hundred years, as the first Silla king surnamed Kim.

Another early Silla king, named Naemul (traditionally r. 356–402), who is remembered as an important ancestor of Silla nobles and kings in the *History of the Three Kingdoms*, was not advanced as an important ancestor to Silla sovereigns until the late Silla (780–935) and early Koryŏ (918–1392) periods since his name appears for the first time in extant epigraphy in 939, four years after Silla's demise. Kim Pusik repurposed a passage from the now lost *History of the Former Qin* (*Qin shu*), likely excerpted in Du You's (735–812) *Encyclopedic History of Institutions* (*Tongdian*), that refers to an otherwise unknown Silla ruler called Nuhan (Louhan in Chinese) dispatching an emissary to northern China in the year 381 – in order to provide material for Naemul's annals in the year 382.

Pak Hyŏkkŏse, the founder first mentioned in the *History of the Three Kingdoms*, is probably a creation of the twelfth century, the time of Kim Pusik, or perhaps a little before, because references to kings of Silla surnamed Pak do not appear in the extant epigraphic record until the mid-twelfth century – and thus well after the fall of the dynasty – and early Chinese historical sources do not report that any ruler of Silla was surnamed Pak. Pak Hyŏkkŏse also has a double: the legendary founder of the Kyŏngju Kim descent group, Alchi (traditionally b. 60). According to *Memorabilia of the Three Kingdoms*, Alchi descended to earth from heaven when a purple cloud engulfed First Forest, and, when it dispersed, a chest of yellow gold hung from a tree. A white chicken cried,

Silla old tomb complex (Taerŭngwŏn), Kyŏngju, 5th–6th century.

heralding the arrival of this baby boy, who stood up and walked around on the fourth day of the eighth lunar month (like the story of the historical Buddha's birth on the eighth day of the fourth lunar month). The legend says, 'Because it was just like the old story of Hyŏkkŏse, for this reason, it is said that he was named Alchi.' Additionally, one of Pak Hyŏkkŏse's titles preserved in this text includes the name/title Alchi, so there is a definite connection between the two.

Origins of the 'Three Kingdoms' in the Third to Fourth Centuries CE

Among the ancient Korean kingdoms, Koguryŏ most likely began to form in the first century BCE. The legendary account of Chumong glosses over what must have been a more complex process. Numerous scholarly theories exist attempting to account for the extant archaeological evidence, because it does not support the simple account of an outside force establishing itself as the ruling elite in the area. For instance, Puyŏ nobles and royalty were buried in the ground in wooden coffins, while early Koguryŏ ruling elites were buried in stone cairns piled into mounds. If the founders of Koguryŏ descended from the ruling Puyŏ family, would they not continue its mortuary traditions? The Chinese *Monograph on the Three Kingdoms*, compiled in the third century, reports that Koguryŏ was a 'separate stock' of Puyŏ, suggesting that it comprised a part of the Puyŏ polity and bore some similarities but was also distinct. Koguryŏ first emerged in the area of the present-day city of Huanren on the Hun river, north of the Yalu river. Already by about the fourth century BCE, however, a predecessor to Koguryŏ, the Yemaek people, had developed as a polity in this same area ruled by a certain Namnyŏ, the lord of the Ye. Chinese records report that he held sway over a population of 280,000. A more likely scenario is that Puyŏ expanded southward and encompassed the Huanren region – called Cholbon Puyŏ in the foundation myth – and later the Chinese instituted the Xuantu commandery in 75 BCE, perhaps to force a wedge between Puyŏ and the emerging, formative Koguryŏ polity between the first century BCE and the second

Iron armour, Kyŏngju, 4th century CE.

century CE. Because all the extant versions of the Koguryŏ founding myth date to the early fifth century CE or later, after the destruction of Puyŏ in 346, it is likely that the emergence of Koguryŏ was an entirely indigenous formation and that memories of exchange relations and political expediency caused the Koguryŏ royal family to draw legitimacy by forging connections to this ancient non-Chinese state by claiming Puyŏ's founding myth as its own.

The origins of Paekche, Kaya and Silla are likewise connected to earlier polities on the Korean peninsula. The *Monograph on the Three Kingdoms* refers to Three Han (Samhan) polities: Mahan, which changed into Paekche; Chinhan, which evolved into Silla; and Pyŏnhan, which developed into the Kaya confederacy. Each of the Three Han comprised numerous walled-town polities that held sway over a largely agrarian populace. Chinese dynastic histories and archaeological finds largely support the idea that the early Paekche state emerged in the late third century CE in the southeastern area of present-day Seoul, south of the Han river. Archaeological evidence has been found at such sites as the P'ungnap earthen fortress. Many Paekche tombs have been excavated in Sŏkch'ondong in Seoul, the earliest of which date to the third century CE. The exteriors of some tumuli in Sŏkch'ondong, believed to be early Paekche tombs, dating to the early fourth century CE, on the outside look like Koguryŏ tombs in Kungnaesŏng (present-day Ji'an), but the interiors are completely different. Did early Paekche rulers and nobles know what Koguryŏ tombs looked like on the outside, but not on the inside? Scholars basing themselves primarily on literary accounts have advanced theories that Paekche was founded by elites from either Puyŏ or Koguryŏ in about 290, to account for the assertions of descent from Puyŏ. However, an equally compelling argument can be made regarding the indigenous development of the small Paekche polity originally based in south Seoul into the early Paekche kingdom. Its assertion of descent from Puyŏ through Koguryŏ functioned to justify its new, grander status because of the importance of the historical memory of Puyŏ.

TWO

KOGURYŎ AND PAEKCHE

Koguryŏ and Paekche were the first two of the ancient Korean kingdoms to develop into sophisticated states. This was because they had direct access to and relatively consistent interstate relations with mainland Chinese polities. Koguryŏ's relationships with Chinese states were typically turbulent because the state was hedged in by Puyŏ to the north and Chinese commanderies to the south and west. By the early first century CE, Koguryŏ was a federated kingdom composed of five tribes. Its king was likely elected by a council of nobles and ratified by the Han state with the title *wang* ('king'), which serves as evidence of Koguryŏ's growth as a state. The relative balance of power in Northeast Asia struck by the Han dynasty by means of offering titles, seals, gifts and Chinese-manufactured goods to conciliatory petty kings and tribal chieftains through its commanderies was weakened when the usurper Wang Mang (45 BCE–23 CE) seized power in 9 CE and established the Xin dynasty. The Koguryŏ king accepted the seal of authority offered by Wang Mang soon after his ascension to the throne. Later, although Wang conscripted Koguryŏ soldiers for a campaign against the Xiongnu in 12 CE, the Koguryŏ men fled en route to the battlefield. Wang punished Koguryŏ by demoting its king to the rank of marquis, luring him to a conference and executing him, and by changing the official name from Koguryŏ ('High Guryŏ') to Haguryŏ ('Low Guryŏ'). Wang's advisers predicted that Koguryŏ and other tribal peoples would rebel against Chinese control, which was proved correct.

Militant Koguryŏ and Its Position in Northeast Asia

After rising along the Hun river and transitioning to the middle reaches of the Yalu (Amnok) river, Koguryŏ gradually expanded the territory under its control and steadily assimilated or held sway over the various peoples of the region during the first centuries of the Common Era. During the suspiciously long 68-year reign of King T'aejo (the 'grand ancestor' or 'grand progenitor', trad. 53–121), kingship became hereditary and more autocratic and centralized. Koguryŏ was thus poised to expand outward in all directions towards the great river basins of the Liao to the west, the Songhua to the north, the Ch'ŏngch'ŏn and Taedong to the south, and the coastal regions of the Eastern Ye and Okchŏ to the southeast. In the autumn of 56, Koguryŏ attacked and assimilated the Eastern Okchŏ, which accounts place in the region of the Kaema mountains in the present-day North Korean provinces of Ryanggang and North Hamgyŏng. Chinese documents of the Han period conventionally referred to the peoples of the northeast using the terms Ye (Hui in Chinese), Maek (Mo in Chinese) and Yemaek (Huimo in Chinese). Although the people of Koguryŏ were one grouping within this broad designation, sometimes Maek is used to refer to Koguryŏ specifically, and at other times the Ye or Yemaek people are said to be partners with Koguryŏ. The Koguryŏ annals report, for instance, that Koguryŏ looted Xuantu commandery in alliance with the Yemaek in 111 and again attacked Hwaryŏ Fortress with the Yemaek in 118. The Eastern Ye peoples, who were likely Tungusic-speaking tribal ancestors of the Malgal, were scattered on the northeastern coast of the Korean peninsula, in present-day South Hamgyŏng and Kangwŏn provinces, centred on Wŏnsan.

The Later Han dynasty attempted to contain Koguryŏ's growth by encouraging Xianbei tribes and Puyŏ to go against it. In 136, for instance, the Puyŏ king visited Luoyang, the great capital of the Later Han, and was entertained lavishly. When Later Han began to falter and lost effective control over the empire in 189, Gongsun Du, lord of the Liaodong commandery, became independent of Han control and held sway over the region. He formed a marriage alliance with Puyŏ. In 204 his son Gongsun Kang

(r. 204–*c.* 220) defeated Koguryŏ and forced it to move its capital, and soon thereafter, perhaps in 206, he established the Daifang commandery on the estuary of the Han river to administer the tribal Korean states to the south through it instead of further north in Lelang.

During the reign of Koguryŏ king Sansang (197–226), a failed power struggle at court led the king's brother, Palgi, to flee with his followers to the Gongsun family in Liaodong. After Gongsun Kang saved his rule over Liaodong by submitting to the warlord Cao Cao (*c.* 155–220), Koguryŏ reached out to both the Sun Wu (222–80) and Cao Wei (220–66) kingdoms during the turbulent first quarter of the third century. Although Koguryŏ assisted Wei by sending troops to support the Chinese state's successful bid to assimilate Liaodong into its empire in 238, the traditional pattern of conflict between Koguryŏ and its Chinese neighbour to the east re-emerged when Wei attempted to re-establish control of the south through Lelang commandery. Koguryŏ attacked Xi'anping in the Liaodong commandery in 242, and Wei retaliated two years later by sacking the Koguryŏ capital at Kungnaesŏng. Another Wei expedition eastward in 245 almost concluded with the capture of Koguryŏ king Tongch'ŏn (r. 227–47), who escaped successfully eastward into the former Okchŏ region.

Puyŏ fortuitously protected itself from Koguryŏ's predatory invasions by maintaining tribute relations with and supporting whatever Chinese power occupied the Liadong region. The Cao Wei dynasty was replaced by the Western Jin (265–317) in 265, but the ruling Sima family's sway in the north had deteriorated by 290. The nature of interstate relations in Northeast Asia was most influenced by the rise of the pastoral Xianbei peoples, and it was the various Yan states established consecutively by the Murong tribes of the Xianbei among the 'five barbarians' (*wuhu* in Chinese) in northern China that caused the southward expansion of Koguryŏ. The Murong Xianbei attacked Puyŏ and killed its king in 285, and continued to harass this beleaguered kingdom in the north until it fell completely in 346. Koguryŏ was relatively successful in deterring Xianbei invasions in the early fourth century and capitalized on the weakened state of the Western Jin by seizing

Xi'anping in Liaodong in 311 and the whole of the Lelang and Daifang commanderies in 313. These conquests brought Koguryŏ into more direct contact with Paekche, which had recently emerged on the southern side of the Han river basin, and had territorial ambitions of its own.

The power of the Murong Xianbei continued to rise in northern China and Manchuria. In 330 Koguryŏ sent emissaries to the Later Zhao dynasty (319–51), in hopes of finding an ally against the Murong. All through the 330s Koguryŏ and the Murong engaged in heated competition over the Liao river basin. Murong Huang (297–348), Prince of Yan, whose son Murong Jun (319–360) would claim the title 'emperor' and found the Former Yan (337–70) in 352, sacked the Koguryŏ capital at Kungnaesŏng in 342 and reduced it to rubble in a most savage manner. They torched the palaces and great houses, plundered ancestral treasures, despoiled and looted royal tombs and took the king's mother as hostage. A few years later, in 346, the Murong conquered Puyŏ and made prisoners of the Puyŏ king and 50,000 of its people.

Koguryŏ maintained an uneasy peace with the Former Yan, which enjoyed dominion over the Liaodong region, until it was destroyed in 370 by Fu Jian (337–385), the most able ruler of the

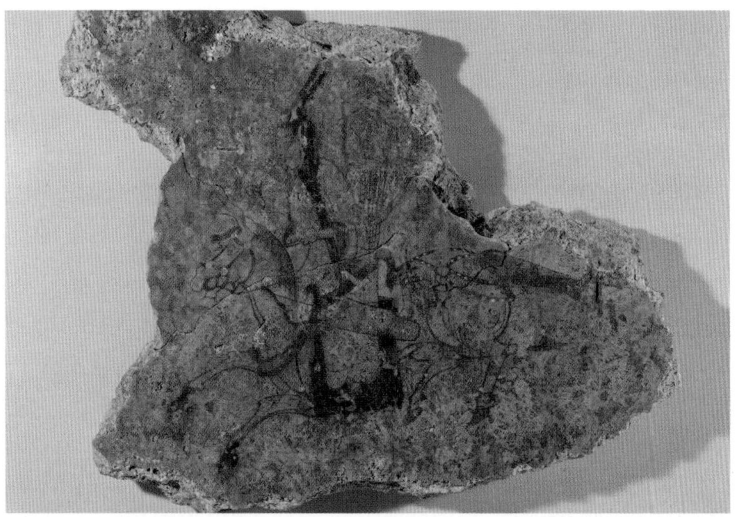

Fragment of tomb mural featuring mounted warrior, Ssangyong Tomb, Koguryŏ, *c.* 250–400 CE.

Bodhisattva statue from Wŏnori monastery site, Koguryŏ, 6th century, clay.

Former Qin dynasty (351–94), founded by the proto-Tibetan Di people of western China. Meanwhile, Koguryŏ struggled with Paekche to the south, which had also set its sights on obtaining hegemony over the area of modern P'yŏngyang, which had served both as the heartland of Old Chosŏn and as the Lelang commandery. Paekche attacked Koguryŏ's stronghold at P'yŏngyang in 371, aided by Wa allies. Koguryŏ king Kogugwŏn (r. 331–71) was killed by a stray arrow in this decisive clash, and it is likely that Koguryŏ lost the walled city as well.

The death of King Kogugwŏn was a great setback to Koguryŏ's growth. In the late fourth century, Koguryŏ was bordered by the Ch'ŏn mountain range to the west, the Northern Puyŏ region (the modern Jilin area) to the north, and the area just north of the Taedong river to the south. Many Chinese immigrants and refugees from the wars in Northeast Asia flocked to Koguryŏ. Chinese influences are reflected in Anak Tomb no. 3, dating to 357, and in the Tŏkhŭngni Old Tumuli, dating to 408. Evidence of Chinese settlers in Koguryŏ is found in wall paintings in the Tongni Tomb, the Tomb of Chang Mui in Pongsan County and the Tomb of Mr Chang in Noamni in Anak County.

King Kogugwŏn's successor, King Sosurim (r. 371–84), instituted several reforms that transformed Koguryŏ by means of adopting and adapting cultural practices and trends from the East Asian mainland. First, in 372, Former Qin emperor Fu Jian sent the monk Shundao (Sundo in Korean) to Koguryŏ with a Buddhist statue and scriptures. Sosurim accepted his liege lord's invitation to embrace the Buddhadharma and made Buddhism a state religion. In 375 the first two monasteries were constructed in the Koguryŏ capital. The style of Mahāyāna Buddhism that entered Koguryŏ emphasized veneration of the future Buddha Maitreya and magico-religious practices promising wealth, health and blessings. The Koryŏ-period compiler of *Memorabilia of the Three Kingdoms*, the monk Iryŏn, felt that the Chinese monk Tanshi (Tamsi in Korean; *fl.* 396–451) of the Northern Wei, a native of Chang'an, who was active in Liaodong for twenty years, was the monk responsible for spreading Buddhism to Koguryŏ in the late fourth and early fifth centuries. Second, also in 372, he established a State Academy (*t'aehak*) in which to train noble youths. The following year, 373, he reportedly promulgated administrative and penal codes. Although none of these laws have been preserved, they were likely influenced by the codes compiled by the Western Jin in 267 and suggest a greater level of sophistication and systematization in Koguryŏ's government administration. Third, Sosurim authorized the compilation of a historical document called *Preserved Records* (*Yugi*), in one hundred rolls. Although lost, some of its contents probably preserved earlier versions of the Koguryŏ founding myth and other stories, such as those found in the *History of the Northern Wei* and the *History of the Three Kingdoms*.

Early Paekche to 475

The Chinese *Monograph on the Three Kingdoms* reports that the Mahan king frequently sent tribute-bearing emissaries to the Western Jin court in 280. However, by the year 300, the Revolt of the Eight Princes had led to the dissolution of the Western Jin and the weakening of their hold over Chinese commanderies on the Korean peninsula. Koguryŏ's destruction of the Lelang and Daifang commanderies in 313–14 provided the context for the emergence of Paekche in the late third and early fourth centuries in the fertile Han river basin. Paekche would eventually become the most powerful and sophisticated of the Three Han polities during the fourth century. The origins of Paekche are shrouded in mystery. In the previous chapter I mentioned a few of the positions advanced by scholars because there is no outside corroborative evidence of the founding of Paekche in the late first century BCE and no mention of the state in Chinese historiography until between 290 and 384 CE. Although the *History of the Three Kingdoms* reports that Paekche king Koi (r. 234–86) established six ministerial posts and instituted a bureaucratic rank system of sixteen levels in 260, there is no supporting evidence of such titles in either epigraphy or historiography until the late sixth and early seventh centuries. The bureaucratic system was likely accomplished by emending and expanding the system developed by Koguryŏ.

By the mid-fourth century, Paekche kings had become rulers of a centralized state and begun to expand in all directions. Paekche established a system of walled cities and settlements, and prestige goods and property apparently bestowed by the Paekche court on local headmen in return for tribute and military aid have been excavated from tombs. Paekche-style gilt-bronze crowns have been discovered in at least eight locations and Paekche-style metalwork has been found in fifteen locations in Paekche territory in the southwestern Korean peninsula, stretching from Wŏnch'ŏlli, in the region northeast of Seoul, all the way down to Kilturi, near Kohŭng, on Namnae Island on the southern coast. This distribution of crowns suggests a means by which Paekche kings rewarded tribal rulers who submitted to their rule and assimilated them into their emerging culture. The greatest challenge to Paekche expansion to the north was Koguryŏ, which Paekche encountered as both struggled to incorporate the territory of the former Daifang commandery.

Paekche kings also extended their influence to the Wa state in early Japan. Both Paekche and the Kaya federation were actively engaged in the oceangoing trade route that linked mainland East Asia with Japan. In 369 Paekche gifted a seven-branched sword, 74.9 centimetres (30 in.) in length, which is presently preserved in the Isono Kami Shrine in Nara, Japan. A translation of the inscription on the sword reads as follows:

> *Front*: At noonday on *pyŏngo*, the sixteenth day of the fifth month of the fourth year of the Taihe reign period [6 July 369], [we] made this seven-branched sword by forging iron a hundred times. [This sword] is able to prevent a hundred [disasters of] war, and is suitably given to marquises and kings. [Three sinographs missing] made.
> *Back*: There has never been a sword like this since the time of our forefathers. The Crown Prince of Paekche remarkably produced it by means of the words of the sage; hence, it was made by royal order for the Wa king. Hand it down and display it to later generations.

Paekche sent this sword before re-establishing relations with the Eastern Jin in 372. The shape and inscription suggest Daoist influence. There has been much scholarly debate about what the presentation of the sword suggests about the

Paekche seven-branched sword (*Ch'ilchido*), 4th century CE, gilt bronze.

relationship between Wa and Paekche. The conventional interpretation, advanced during the colonial period in the first half of the twentieth century, is that the sword was an offering presented or dedicated as tribute from a lesser state to a greater state. However, this does not tally with the actual language of the inscription, which suggests that the giver was in a higher position. For instance, if the Wa were conceptualized as superior to Paekche, the expression 'marquises and kings' would not likely have been used, as well as the command to show it to later generations. Thus Korean scholars tend to understand that the sword was bestowed by Paekche on their Wa allies as a gift.

Like Koguryŏ, Paekche also adopted Buddhism as a state religion in the late fourth century. The Serindian monk Maranant'a was dispatched by the Eastern Jin to the Paekche court, by sea, in 384. Although it is possible that Buddhist monks arrived in Paekche by sea prior to Maranant'a, no documentary or archaeological evidence of Buddhism in the Paekche domain has been confirmed until the fifth century. The *History of the Three Kingdoms* reports that Paekche king Kŭn Kusu (r. 375–84) constructed a monastery in Hansŏng (Seoul) and had ten monks ordained to inaugurate the religion in his kingdom.

King Kwanggaet'o and Koguryŏ's Age of Southward Expansion

Interstate relations ebbed and flowed freely in late fourth-century Northeast Asia. The short-lived Later Yan (384–407) state controlled the Liaodong plain in the 380s, but its leader, Murong Chui (326–396), was defeated utterly by Northern Wei military forces in 395 at the Battle of Canhepo. To the south, Koguryŏ fought heated offensive and defensive confrontations with Paekche in the area of the Yesŏng river. To the north, the Khitans (Qidan in Chinese) plundered the border regions of Koguryŏ and Later Yan. In addition, the Wa, in league with Paekche, meddled in the affairs of the Kaya kingdoms and applied pressure to Silla. Hedged in and suffering attacks by enemies, the Silla king requested relief from Koguryŏ in 392 and sent Crown Prince Silsŏng (d. 417) as a hostage.

In these circumstances, Koguryŏ king Kwanggaet'o (374–413; r. 391–413) piloted his people to resounding success on multiple fronts. He first attacked and subdued Paekche, and then made a decisive expedition against the Khitans, chastising them by capturing three villages, which engendered the release of more than 10,000 people of Koguryŏ who had been detained by the Khitans. He organized a large-scale attack on Paekche in 396, capturing 58 strongholds in the lower reaches of the Han river basin, and received the submission of the Paekche king. However, in 397, Paekche king Asin (r. 392–405) sent his heir apparent, Chŏnji, to Wa and concluded a treaty of mutual friendship to resist being dominated by Koguryŏ. Additionally, Wa and their allies in the Kaya states started an offensive against Silla in 399. The Silla king requested troops, and Koguryŏ responded in the year 400 by sending 50,000 combined forces of infantry and cavalry. The Koguryŏ troops marched down southward along the Naktong river basin, expelling the Kaya forces, and then over to the Silla capital, ejecting the Wa invaders in a great rout. However, while the Koguryŏ military was busy on the southern part of the peninsula, the Later Yan captured two fortresses and seized 5,000 households. As a result of their southward expedition, Koguryŏ exerted much influence on Silla, and Kwanggaet'o appears to have established a protectorate over the young Silla state that lasted for much of the fifth century. Evidence for this is found in the inscription on the Chungwŏn Koguryŏ stele, which I date to 480–81, which refers to the Silla king as the '*maegŭm* [paramount chieftain] of the Eastern Barbarians', and to the two states as having an older-brother–younger-brother relationship, suggesting that Koguryŏ viewed itself as a civilized centre in Northeast Asia surrounded by quasi-civilized satellite countries. It also refers to Koguryŏ military advisers posted to Silla called 'banner authorities within Silla lands' (*Silla t'onae tangju*).

After chastising Paekche and its Wa Japanese allies, Kwanggaet'o turned his gaze westward to reckon with the Later Yan, which had taken advantage of Koguryŏ's southward expedition. During the first decade of the 400s, Koguryŏ annexed lands east of the Liao river, including Liaodong Fortress in 405. In 407 Gao Yun (Ko Un, *fl.* 407–9), a warrior of Koguryŏ extraction serving the Later Yan, usurped the throne and established the short-lived Northern Yan dynasty (407–36). Kwanggaet'o dispatched emissaries offering congratulations and amicable relations, and Gao responded favourably. Even after Gao was assassinated in 409, his successor, Feng Ba (d. 430), continued the cordial association between the two states due to the powerful Northern Wei dynasty (386–534) that held sway over most of northern China.

Kwanggaet'o's son and successor, King Changsu (r. 413–91), erected a giant stele near Kwanggaet'o's tumuli, the inscription on which records Kwanggaet'o accomplishments in 1,800 sinographs carved in intaglio. The four-sided stone, approximately 6.39 metres (21 ft) high, exists *in situ* in modern Tonggou, near the old Koguryŏ capital of Kungnaesŏng (modern Ji'an, in Jilin prefecture). It reports that Kwanggaet'o had conquered 64 walled towns and fortresses and 1,400 villages and settlements by the time of his death at age 39.

Koguryŏ bowl with *Hou* inscription, 415 CE, bronze.

Changsu forged diplomatic relations with the Northern Wei, which had been founded by the Tuoba (Tabgach) Xianbei and conquered the Later Yan and the Northern Yan and all the other states in northern China. He also developed a relationship with the Rouran Khaganate in the northern steppes. Changsu's foreign relations effectively counterbalanced Paekche's relations with southern Chinese dynasties. With the western and northern border areas stabilized, Changsu moved his capital from Kungnaesŏng to P'yŏngyang in 427. Over the course of thirty years, the Koguryŏ royal family had invested much wealth in preparing P'yŏngyang. Kwanggaet'o established nine monasteries there in 393, and the new capital and the walled Anhak Palace were protected by three fortresses: Taesŏng Mountain Fortress to the north; Kobang Mountain Fortress to the south, just north of the Taedong river; and Ch'ŏngam Fortress to the west, just north of Rŭngna Island and Taech'wi Island in the P'ae river.

Detail of Koguryŏ envoy (left) in *Liang Tribute Register* (*Wanghuitu*), *c.* 552–4 CE, ink on paper scroll.

Detail of Paekche envoy (centre) in *Liang Tribute Register* (*Wanghuitu*), *c.* 552–4 CE, ink on paper scroll.

Paekche was the country most threatened by the movement of Koguryŏ's capital to P'yŏngyang. The *History of the Three Kingdoms* reports that, in 433, Paekche sent an embassy to Silla requesting the resumption of amicable relations between the two states, and the Silla annals confirm that the request was accepted. Both sides utilized this mutual alliance against Koguryŏ and responded to calls for aid against Koguryŏ incursions for the remainder of the fifth century. For the next several decades, Koguryŏ abstained from large-scale invasion of Paekche; it merely engaged in scattered skirmishes and forays along its southern border. In 475, however, Changsu unleashed a powerful expeditionary force of 30,000 that conquered the Paekche capital at Hansŏng, in the southeastern region of modern Seoul. Paekche king Kaero (r. 455–75) was executed, perhaps as revenge for the death of Koguryŏ king Kogugwŏn a century before in the Battle of P'yŏngyang. Paekche prince Munju (r. 475–77), who was dispatched to seek aid from Silla, succeeded his father to the throne.

Koguryŏ followed up this decisive victory by advancing its southern frontiers to the southern edge of the Gulf of Namyang (near Hwasŏng, south of Inch'ŏn) on the west and Chungnyŏng (Bamboo Pass) on the east. In essence, Koguryŏ controlled the regions north of the Ch'aryŏng and Sobaek mountain ranges, applying pressure to Paekche, Kaya and Silla. As a result of this expansion, Changsu established secondary capitals at Kungnaesŏng and Hansŏng, in Chaeryŏng county in modern Hwanghae province, and reorganized the country into five provinces.

The Resurgence of Paekche in Ungjin and Sabi

In the aftermath of Koguryŏ's success in subjugating the whole of the Han river basin, Paekche was forced to remove its capital to Ungjin, present-day Kongju, in South Ch'ungch'ŏng province, which enjoyed abundant natural defences. After a coup engineered by chief counsellors to place the son of Munju's younger brother Konji on the throne, King Tongsŏng (r. 479–501), who had been a hostage in Yamato Japan prior to his assumption of the throne, guided his country through difficult times. He rebuilt strongholds and fortresses along his borders, and dispatched military aid to Silla when Koguryŏ and sometimes Malgal units attacked Silla's borders in 481, 484 and 494. Paekche requested a marriage alliance with Silla in 493, and a woman of noble blood became a secondary wife of Tongsŏng. Silla sent support troops to assist Paekche during a Koguryŏ incursion in 495. In 498 Tongsŏng reasserted Paekche's interest in and control over the natives of T'amna (Cheju Island), which was then still an independent polity. However, he was killed by an assassin's knife.

Paekche recovered from its military weakness of the previous century under the guidance of the mature King Muryŏng (r. 501–23), who was a son either of Tongsŏng or of Kaero. Nevertheless, his early reign was rocky, as he had to put down an uprising incited by Paek Ka, the rebellious minister of the royal garrisons who was responsible for the regicide of Tongsŏng. Although Koguryŏ and its Malgal allies harassed their northern borders, Paekche gained strength by pursuing relations with the cultured Liang dynasty

(502–57) in southern China. Muryŏng dispatched his first tribute mission in 512, and, as a result of the second mission in 521, he was recognized as king of Paekche. Paekche's military had recovered sufficiently to the extent that Muryŏng incorporated parts of Kaya into Paekche in 512–13. Muryŏng was strongly influenced by the model of Liang emperor Wu (r. 502–49), who was a fervent devotee of Buddhism. Adherence to Buddhism became significant in Paekche politics and culture from this time forward. The Liang-style lotus motif found on the bricks of King Muryŏng's tomb attests to the significance of Buddhism in the legitimation of Paekche rulers.

The close relationship between the Buddhist church and the Liang state continued to influence Paekche into the reign of King Sŏng (Sŏngmyŏng, r. 523–54). Sŏng erected in the capital, Ungjin, a large monastery, Taet'ong Monastery, which symbolized the close relationship between the church and state – being named after Liang emperor Wu's Datong reign era (527–9). Paekche's relations with Silla deteriorated due to the latter's increased military capacity and Silla resentment over Paekche's annexation of some Kaya territory in 540. In 538 Sŏng relocated the capital to Sabi, present-day Puyŏ, 30 kilometres (19 mi.) southwest of Ungjin, to be closer to the richly productive agricultural land as well as the Kŭm river, which was the state's lifeline for diplomacy and trade. Sŏng officially changed his country's name to 'South Puyŏ', but the new moniker never caught on. Although the Liang emperor recognized Sŏng as king of Paekche in 524, Sŏng only sent three tribute-bearing missions to the southern Chinese dynasty: in 534, 541 and 549. The mission of 541 is significant in that Sŏng requested painters, artisans, a specialist in the *Book of Songs* (*Shi jing*) and commentaries to Buddhist sūtras. In 548 Koguryŏ attacked a Paekche fortress; Sŏng called to Silla for aid, and Silla king Chinhŭng (r. 540–76) rapidly dispatched a relief army that soundly defeated the invading host. This would be the last time Silla could be counted on as an ally.

Paekche's relations with Yamato Japan traditionally had been close, but internal disturbances in Japan contributed to the erosion of Yamato influence in Paekche beginning in the latter part of the

Roof-end tile with lotus design, Paekche, 6th century CE.

fifth century. Contact appears to have rebounded by the late 530s and, later in his reign, Sŏng increasingly turned to Yamato for aid, particularly war materiel. Japanese records show a continual stream of hostages being sent to Japan, demonstrating Paekche's needs. Sometime in the mid-sixth century, Sŏng dispatched Buddhist monks to Yamato to encourage the island kingdom to adopt the religion. The eighth-century *Chronicles of Japan* (*Nihon shōki*) provides the date of 552, and the *Origins of Gangōji* (*Gangōji engi*) and other texts advance the year 538. Japanese scholars have challenged the traditional date of 552 because they believe it was selected merely for being the first year of the 'decline of the Dharma [Buddhist teaching]' (*mappō* in Japanese), but recent scholarship has questioned the reliability of the year 538 as well. Regardless, by the 550s, Paekche Buddhist monks served as hostages in Japan even before Buddhism was officially recognized by the Yamato court, attesting to the importance of Buddhism in Paekche culture and society.

In 550 Silla king Chinhŭng waited until the forces of Koguryŏ and Paekche had exhausted themselves in a series of engagements and then seized for himself the two strongholds that were in contention – one of which formerly had been Paekche's. In 551 Paekche planned to retake an extensive area on the northern bank of the Han river, including Hansŏng, in a major offensive. Silla putatively dispatched reinforcements but used them to occupy a large area of Koguryŏ in what is present-day Kangwŏn province. In 553 Silla seized more Paekche territory and wrested control of Paekche's recently re-won area in the Han river basin, enabling it to secure direct access to the Yellow Sea and the Chinese states beyond. In 554 Sŏng sought to mount a punitive expedition against

Earthenware tile with cloud design from Oeri, Puyŏ, Paekche, 6th–7th century CE.

Silla, but his invading force was ambushed en route and he was killed.

In the second half of the sixth century, Paekche struggled militarily, but strove to build its relationship with Yamato Japan in the three official missions sent between 555 and 575. While the status of Buddhism was contested on the archipelago, Paekche king Widŏk (r. 554–98) sent Buddhist texts in 577 and a larger contingent of Buddhist relics, literate and skilled monks, and artisans in 588. Paekche's wealth and fortunes began to improve in 600, when King Pŏp (r. 599–600) began work on the massive Wanghŭng Monastery in the capital.

King Mu (r. 600–641) brought about the final resurgence of Paekche in the first half of the seventh century. Although his reign started with an unsuccessful attack on Silla's Amak Mountain Fortress in 602, he followed up with successful attacks on Silla in 616, 623, 624 and 626–7, in which he took possession of several fortresses. Mu also reached out to the powerful Sui dynasty (581–618) in 607, requesting an attack on Koguryŏ, and sent tribute in 608 and 614. Mu was hesitant to recognize the Tang dynasty, when it replaced the Sui amid numerous rebellions and unrest in China. He did not send tribute until 621, and in 624 the Tang confirmed Mu's royal status. Mu dispatched ten missions to Tang between 625 and 639; and both Paekche and Silla denounced Koguryŏ to the Tang court in 626. However, Silla had Tang emperor Taizong (r. 627–49) censure Paekche for its attacks in 627. Despite Taizong's warning, Mu made four successful attacks on Silla between 628 and 641, while Silla was on the defensive, having only attempted incursions into Paekche in 605 and 618 at Kajam Fortress. Wanghŭng Monastery was completed in 634, and Mu sent students to Chang'an, the Tang capital, to study at the Institute for the Veneration of Literature (*chongwenguan*) in 639.

King Mu seems to have become a legendary figure in his own time. The Koryŏ monk Iryŏn preserved a mythical account of his birth: he was said to be the product of a lonely widow and a dragon resident in a lake near her humble dwelling. As a boy named Sŏdong (Mattung), he supported his mother by digging and selling sweet potatoes. Hearing of the beauty of a Silla princess prone to fits of crying, he used the children who ate his sweet potatoes to spread a rumour of an amorous encounter between himself and the princess preserved in a short native song (*hyangga*):

> Princess Sŏnhwa
> Secretly had an illicit affair;
> Furtively embracing and leaving
> Sŏdong's room at night.[5]

This caused the princess to be expelled from the palace, where, reportedly, Sŏdong married her and took her back to Paekche before ascending the throne. Although this is a beloved story of ancient Korea, the truth is that Mu did not marry a Silla princess: an inscription on a gold plate excavated from the site of Mirŭk Monastery attests to the more plausible fact that his wife was the daughter of a high-ranking Paekche minister (*chwap'yŏng*) named Sat'aek Chŏktŏk. Other narratives preserved by Iryŏn deal with the site of Mirŭk Monastery in Iksan, which must have been the site of a new capital proposed by Mu. The function of the monastery was to firmly link Paekche to the future Buddha Maitreya. The ground plan of the monastery recreated the three assemblies in which Maitreya will preach the Buddhadharma after attaining Buddhahood in the distant future, thus suggesting that Mu sought to legitimate his rule by presenting Paekche as the very place where the future Buddha will re-establish the Buddhist teaching.

The final ruler of Paekche, King Ŭija (r. 641–60), continued the military success enjoyed by Mu, capturing more than forty Silla fortresses in 642. Of these, the Taeya Fortress in the middle of the old Kaya territory was the most significant because the daughter and son-in-law of the Silla noble and statesman Kim Ch'unch'u (604–661) were killed in the fray. In 643 Paekche and Koguryŏ reached a joint agreement to attack Silla's Tanghang Fortress, which guarded its access to China via the Yellow Sea. Although Silla general Kim Yusin (595–673) was briefly successful in 644 in retaking some strongholds that had fallen to Paekche, Ŭija's military efforts continued to be effective against Silla to the extent that, in 651, Silla had Tang emperor Gaozong (r. 649–83) send a rescript to Ŭija

Court ladies jumping from the 'Rock of Falling Flowers' at the fall of the Paekche capital in 660 CE, mural, Nakhwaam, Puyŏ.

censuring him for the seizure of strategic forts, impeding Silla's ability to send tribute to Tang. In 655 another joint attack with Koguryŏ and its Malgal confederates took thirty Silla fortifications. Ŭija's last offensive was in 659. On the one hand, the account of Paekche in the *New History of the Tang* preserves an encomium asserting that Ŭija was a paragon of filial piety and calls him the 'Zengzi of Korea'. On the other hand, the *History of the Three Kingdoms* reports that in his later years Ŭija blatantly indulged in excesses and misgovernment, such as granting the high rank of *chwap'yong* to 41 of his sons by concubines. For this reason, the last years of his reign, 659–60, show a preponderance of ill omens. Ŭija continued to enjoy stable military support from Yamato Japan, and some Paekche princes, most notably Prince P'ung, resided in Japan as hostages until Paekche's final collapse in 663 after the Silla–Tang alliance captured the Paekche capital in 660. He died in captivity in Tang after confessing his transgressions before Tang emperor Gaozong.

Koguryŏ's Struggles with Sui and Tang China

In the late fifth century and the early sixth, Koguryŏ kings sought to maintain the balance of power in Northeast Asia by forging relations with the Rouran Khaganate in order to restrain the growth of the Northern Wei. If the Northern Wei attacked the Rouran, it would leave its southern borders open to attack from the Liang, thus keeping the Northern Wei in check. Although Koguryŏ fought a few battles with the Northern Wei, due to the inherent stability brought about by the nature of the political geography, Koguryŏ enjoyed a long period of relative peace on its northern and western borders. Nevertheless, after the Rebellion of the Six Garrisons in 520 shook the stability of the Northern Wei and caused confusion in the Liaoxi region, Koguryŏ king Anjang (r. 519–31) took the opportunity to attack westward and annex territory in the Liaodong region. The Rouran were eventually replaced by their underlings, the Tujue (Türks), who started their gambit for mastery of the steppe in the second lunar month of 552.

Koguryŏ was thrown into confusion over the issue of succession with the illness and passing of King Anwŏn (r. 531–45). A civil war erupted in the winter of 544 that divided the various noble families. Anwŏn had three queens: the first had no offspring, but the second and third each produced one son. Koguryŏ's elite were divided over support for one or the other of these two princes, and the two groups fought over control of the palace city for three days. The supporters of the son of the second queen prevailed, with the death toll reaching 2,000, and he ascended the throne at the tender age of eight, becoming King Yangwŏn (r. 545–59). This internal strife in Koguryŏ provides the context for the success of Silla's conquest of Koguryŏ territory and its takeover of the Han river basin in the 550s.

The founding of the Sui dynasty by Emperor Wen (r. 581–604), and in 589 its reunification of China, which had been divided for four centuries, changed the balance of power in East Asia. Hitherto, Koguryŏ and Paekche had been bitter adversaries, but now they had a common enemy in Silla, which had usurped the rich and strategically important Han river basin. Now surrounded by enemy states, Silla clung tenaciously to its lifeline to the Chinese mainland and cultivated close relations with the dominant power on the continent to protect its territorial holdings by threat of invasion from China. Koguryŏ came into conflict with the Sui because it restricted the Khitan and Malgal peoples' access to Sui through its territories in the Liaodong region.

Koguryŏ king Yŏngyang (r. 590–618) attacked Sui strongholds in Liaoxi in 598 in hopes of stimulating the Tujue to action on Sui's northern borders, but his plan backfired because the Sui forces were successful in subduing both the Eastern and Western Tujue. Although Sui emperor Wen was furious with Koguryŏ, rescinding all official ranks and titles granted to the Koguryŏ king, and planned an invasion, poor weather, hunger and rampant disease decimated the Sui naval and infantry forces, causing the emperor to abandon his punitive expedition. After Sui emperor Yang (r. 604–18) ascended the throne, he decided to subjugate intractable Koguryŏ with an overwhelming expeditionary force. Emperor Yang's early reign was occupied by the completion of the Tongji and Han Canals, which together formed part of the Grand Canal linking the capital, Luoyang, to the grain-rich south via the Huai and Yangzi rivers – at substantial cost of life. Emperor Yang also went on eleven imperial tours, including military campaigns to various regions under his sway. Emperor Yang's invasion of Koguryŏ in 612 was the climax of these imperial campaigns. He personally led an army of more than a million soldiers with an even larger contingent of support and logistics personnel. The supply train is said to have stretched out for 960 *li*, or approximately 310,000 kilometres (192,625 mi.) following the measurement of the *li* in the Tang period. Due to inclement weather and rough terrain, the bulk of the Sui host was unable to advance, so a detachment of 305,000 was dispatched to make a direct assault on P'yŏngyang, bypassing other frontier strongholds in hopes of a quick victory over an unsuspecting capital. Koguryŏ general Ŭlchi Mundŏk fought and lost several skirmishes, luring the Chinese force into a false sense of superiority. Once they reached the walls of P'yŏngyang, General Ŭlchi reportedly sent the leading Sui general Yu Zhongwen (545–612) the following poem:

Your divine plans have probed the patterns of heaven.
Your subtle calculations have fathomed the principles
of earth.
In battle you are victorious, your merit is already great.
Be content and seek to say 'Stop'.[6]

General Yu responded with an admonitory letter, chastising Koguryŏ; but ultimately was forced to retreat because his troops were tired and their supplies were exhausted. When the Chinese troops, making a fighting retreat, were halfway across the Sal river (present-day Ch'ŏngch'ŏn river), General Ŭlchi unleashed the full contingent of his forces and achieved a resounding success. Only 2,700 men made it back to the fortress at Liaodong.

In 613 Sui emperor Yang personally led forces that laid siege to Koguryŏ strongholds in the Liaodong region, but a serious rebellion in the Chinese heartland was an important sign that the Sui was falling apart at the seams. The situation was so bad in China that one of Emperor Yang's top military aides, Vice Minister of War Hu Sizheng (d. 614), fled to Koguryŏ for asylum. After suppressing the rebellion, Emperor Yang sought to invade Koguryŏ again, but Koguryŏ responded with a peace proposal and repatriated Minister Hu as part of the deal. Frustrated at his repeated failures, Emperor Yang vented his spleen on Minister Hu: his body was torn asunder and boiled, his remaining bones were cremated and his ashes were scattered to the four winds. In the end, Sui emperor Yang was assassinated as his empire deteriorated into chaos and rebellion in 618.

The rise of the Tang dynasty in 618 ushered in a period of tentative peace between Koguryŏ and its powerful neighbour. While the Tang consolidated their rule, restored central administration and suppressed lingering opposition at home and resistance among the Tujue on the northern steppe, Koguryŏ king Yŏngnyu (r. 618–42) embarked on an ambitious defensive enterprise: the construction of a thousand-*li* wall along its western border from modern Ningan to the Gulf of Bohai, which took sixteen years to complete. General Yŏn Kaesomun (d. 665), a forceful leader possessing uncompromising views and despotic tendencies, supervised the project and seized power in a *coup d'état* in 642. After placing the tractable King

Paekche incense burner depicting the realm of immortals, Mt Penglai, topped by a phoenix, 6th century CE, gilt bronze.

Pojang (r. 642–68) on the throne, General Yŏn dominated Koguryŏ affairs. In 642, when the Silla noble Kim Ch'unch'u went to Koguryŏ as an emissary seeking aid against Paekche, General Yŏn threw him in prison after demanding the return of Koguryŏ territory annexed by Silla in the 550s. Because Paekche and Koguryŏ schemed to destroy Silla's Tanghang Fortress, Silla turned directly to Tang for aid. General Yŏn also imprisoned the Tang emissary sent to mediate between the two Korean states.

Koguryŏ's rough treatment of the Tang emissary and General Yŏn's takeover of actual power at court provided Tang emperor Taizong with a pretext for an expedition against Koguryŏ in 645. Taizong personally led the invasion force of 170,000, and as a more accomplished strategist than Sui emperor Yang, subdued all major Koguryŏ strongholds and defences, including Koguryŏ's Yodong (Liaodong) Fortress, within a few months. The Tang military machine converged on and laid siege to Ansi Fortress, a small stronghold with an accompanying community of citizens strategically placed on a mountain in the Liaodong peninsula, which scholars suggest is present-day Yingchengzi, south of Haicheng city. Koguryŏ sent a large force of 150,000 reinforcements, including Malgal units, but they were dispersed by the Tang forces. Koguryŏ attempted all means possible, including trying to induce the Xueyantuo (Syr-Tardush) tribe in Outer Mongolia to strike Tang from the rear, to bring relief to the beleaguered troops and people in the fortress – but to no avail. Under the capable leadership of its commander, Ansi Fortress proved too difficult for Tang emperor Taizong to subdue. The invaders tried all manner of offensive tactics, but they were met with improvised defences. The Chinese ultimately built an earthen mound that reached the height of the fortress walls, which took 500,000 labourers two months, but the Koguryŏ defenders merely increased the height of the walls to maintain an advantage. When Taizong counted the cost in human life, supply shortages and most importantly the stealthy advent of cold weather, he grudgingly ordered the army to withdraw. Seeing the Chinese army retreat, the Koguryŏ commander appeared on the wall and bade them farewell. Deeply impressed by their valiance and bravery, the Tang Son of Heaven gifted them with a hundred bolts of silk as a token of his esteem. Taizong organized expeditionary forces again in 647 and 648, but they did not make any substantial headway against Koguryŏ's defences.

House-shaped earthenware excavated in Taegu, Kaya, 4th–5th century CE.

THREE
KAYA AND EARLY SILLA

The Kaya confederacy and the early Silla kingdom emerged in the southeastern sector of the Korean peninsula, protected by the T'aebaek mountain range in the north and the Honam range to the west. Koreans have referred to this area historically as the Yŏngnam region: the land 'south of the passes'. The Naktong river flows southward from the T'aebaek mountains and empties into the sea at present-day Pusan. Many petty states that eventually coalesced into the Kaya confederation were located on the eastern and western shores of the Naktong river, and the western advance of the Silla state, centred on present-day Kyŏngju, eventually made the river the boundary between these two polities. Despite the narrative presented in the twelfth-century *History of the Three Kingdoms*, the Silla kingdom did not fully appear until the fourth century, and it developed in conjunction and competition with the petty states of the Kaya confederacy.

The destruction of the Old Chosŏn state by the Han dynasty at the end of the second century BCE caused the dispersal of refugees throughout the southern part of the Korean peninsula. These migrants seem to have introduced a new archaeological development: earthen-pit tombs. By the first century BCE, the goods excavated from these tombs include black and brown patternless earthenware, lacquerware, double-edged bronze blades in the Old Chosŏn style and other metal goods, including bronze mirrors, iron daggers and bronze horse bells.

The Kaya Confederacy of the Early Period

The 'Kaya confederacy' refers to several walled-city polities that emerged from Pyŏnjin (Pyŏnhan) on the eastern and western sides of the Naktong river basin. They shared a generally common culture in earthenware and weapons and banded together in the early centuries of the Common Era for trade and defence. Although the earthen-pit tombs that archaeologists believe were introduced by migrants fleeing the destruction of Old Chosŏn first appear in Kyŏngju, the future heartland of the Silla kingdom, and Ch'angwŏn, a Pyŏnjin settlement on the lower reaches of the Naktong river, the present-day city of Kimhae quickly replaced Ch'angwŏn as the leading polity of what would become the Kaya confederacy of the early period. In the early centuries CE, the walled-town communities of Chinhan (Silla) and Pyŏnhan (Kaya) developed in close cultural relation. Many of the settlements were so closely entwined that the Chinese first refer to them as Pyŏnjin, suggesting close relations between Chinhan and Pyŏnhan. The 'Account of the Eastern Yi' in the *Monograph on the Three Kingdoms*, which was compiled in the mid-third century, refers to a state called 'Kuya' (believed to be an early version of Kaya) as one of the twelve petty states of Pyŏnjin. This same Chinese record reports that Pyŏnjin supplied iron to Han China, the Ye tribes of the eastern coast of the Korean peninsula and various Wa tribes on the Japanese archipelago, as well as the Lelang and Daifang commanderies. Thus the Kaya confederacy of the early period likely arose in the late third century with the expansion of the iron trade with these groups of peoples.

The archaeological distribution of the slightly absorptive grey-coloured 'tile-quality earthenware' (*wajil t'ogi*), the most representative forms of which are large, globular round-bottomed jars with ox-ear handles and small, flat-bottomed bowls, as well as iron daggers and two-edged bronze spearheads, helps delineate the general territory of the Kaya confederacy of the early period. It encompassed the whole of present-day South Kyŏngsang province save for Ulsan city; and to that can be appended a few regions in North Kyŏngsang province: Koryŏng county, Sŏngju county and

Kimch'ŏn city. This early Kaya confederacy was centred on the lower reaches of the Naktong river, such as Kimhae, Ch'angwŏn, Haman and Pusan, all of which have yielded a wide distribution of remains. The leading Kaya polity was the Karak state in Kimhae.

The Kaya confederation of the early period was dismantled at the height of its influence and prosperity. By the second half of the third century, hard, non-absorbing grey stoneware (*tojil t'ogi*) had replaced tile-quality earthenware as grave goods. In addition, large numbers of iron weapons were also interred. Koguryŏ's annexation of the Lelang and Daifang commanderies unleashed a period of land grabbing and territorial tension on the Korean peninsula. Early on, the Silla and Kaya polities were allied against a group known as the eight polities of P'osang. Although the *History of the Three Kingdoms* reports that P'osang attacked Kaya in 209 CE, and that Silla aided Kaya in resisting the invasion, it likely happened more than a century later in the first half of the fourth century. At this time, the present-day region of Ulsan city, which distributed duck-shaped earthenware and displayed other ties with Kaya culture, fell fully under the jurisdiction of Silla.

Paekche embarked on a period of expansion once King Kŭn Ch'ogo (r. 346–75) ascended the throne. The account of the 49th year of the regency of Jingū (249 CE) in the *Chronicles of Japan* (*Nihon shōki*) reports that Wa armies and Paekche generals subdued seven Kaya polities in the process of attacking Silla. This story was once used to substantiate the position that Wa forces subjugated Kaya

Duck-shaped earthenware, Kaya confederacy, *c.* 4th–6th century CE.

in 369; however, the reliability of this account is now questioned. Another passage in the annals of Kinmei (r. 531–71) in the *Chronicles of Japan* has Paekche king Sŏng (r. 523–54) reminisce about this time, remembering that the chiefs (*kanji*) of various Kaya polities first dispatched emissaries, communicated with each other and formed bonds of friendship. This situation seems closer to the facts. Due to amicable relations with Paekche, the Kaya confederation was able to form a stable and lucrative system of trade as an intermediate base between Paekche and Wa. Meanwhile, Koguryŏ government improved during the reign of King Sosurim (r. 371–84) and friendly relations were established with the Former Qin dynasty (351–94) in northern China, including the official recognition of Buddhism by the Koguryŏ court. Koguryŏ formed relations with Silla, and Silla advanced by adopting and adapting Koguryŏ culture.

The 'Inscription on the Stele Erected in Honour of Koguryŏ King Kwanggaet'o' reports that when Kwanggaet'o heard that Paekche had made an alliance with the Wa, he was gravely concerned. Silla had been overrun by invaders from Paekche, Wa and Kaya. In 399 he first dispatched troops to the walled city of P'yŏngyang and then, in 400, sent 50,000 Koguryŏ troops down to Silla to root out the allied forces of Paekche, Wa and Kaya. Koguryŏ and Silla forces chased the allied invaders from Kaya and Wa to 'Imna Kara' (the Karak state in Kimhae) and surrendered immediately after entering one of their strongholds. As a result of this war, although Silla sent hostages to Koguryŏ and Wa, it survived and superseded Kaya as the hegemonic power in the southeastern Yŏngnam region of the Korean peninsula. Paekche lost its trade network with Wa, and the Karak state in Kimhae lost its pre-eminence among the Kaya polities.

The Kaya Confederacy of the Later Period

Kaya and Silla had developed culturally in tandem in the early centuries of the Common Era. After Koguryŏ's conquest of the Karak state in Kimhae, the cultural area of Kaya and Silla was sundered, and the Silla cultural area developed its own representative style. The regions of Sŏngju, Ch'angnyŏng, Yangsan and

Pusan, which had previously belonged to the Kaya confederacy, voluntarily joined with Silla, and the old tombs in those areas reflect the growing presence of Silla in terms of scale and remains. The Kimhae–Ch'angwŏn region, which had previously been the leading Kaya polity because of its location and control of maritime trade, fell into decline for several decades. The Pallo state in Koryŏng took in migrants and enjoyed high agricultural production. In 442 Chief Kibon of Pallo became connected to Paekche and was recognized as the premier representative of the Kaya area. Kibon utilized this opportunity to reinitiate trade with Wa. In the middle of the fifth century, the Pallo state changed its name to Kara or Tae Kaya ('great Kaya') and organized the petty states in its area, thus forming the Kaya confederation of the late period.

Tae Kaya was dynamic in the second half of the fifth century. It sent tribute to the newly established Southern Qi dynasty in 479, and its king, Haji, was granted a noble title. In 481 Koguryŏ invaded Silla, took seven fortresses and advanced towards present-day P'ohang. Kaya and Paekche dispatched reinforcements to halt the Koguryŏ intrusion. In response, Silla expanded northward and westward and built strongholds inside and outside Ch'up'ungnyŏng (Autumn Wind Pass), the historically strategic mountain pass north of Kimch'ŏn that presently forms the border between the North Ch'ungch'ŏng and North Kyŏngsang provinces. As an expression of goodwill, Kaya gifted Silla with a white pheasant in 496.

Kaya's territory and sphere of influence can be extrapolated from a passage from the *Old Records of Silla* (*Silla kogi*) preserved in the 'Monograph on Music' in the *History of the Three Kingdoms*. It names twelve tunes composed by the master musician Urŭk of Kaya (*fl.* 551), ten of which provide the names of geographic locations in the Kaya domain. These regions include what is presently Koryŏng in North Kyŏngsang province; Kimhae, Sach'ŏn, Kŏch'ang, Ch'ogye and Purim in South Kyŏngsang province; Namwŏn, Pŏnam and Imsil of North Chŏlla province; and Yŏsu and Kwangnyang of South Chŏlla province. It is clear that areas in the Honam region (the two Chŏlla provinces) likely traded with or were influenced by Kaya because Kaya products, such as earthenware, have been excavated as grave goods.

Earthenware cup with mounted warrior, Kaya, 5th century CE.

The Kaya confederation of the late period began to wane when Paekche king Muryŏng (r. 501–23) advanced southward in 512 to incorporate the eastern part of the Honam region. Evidence of the Paekche conquest is found in the archaeological record: tomb mounds in Kwangyang, Yŏsu and Sunch'ŏn, which date to the second half of the sixth century, changed from Kaya-style earthen pit tombs to Paekche-style earthen pit tombs. Paekche mountain fortresses were also constructed in these areas. In 514 Kaya responded by building strongholds of its own to halt the Paekche advance; and in 522 it requested a marriage alliance with Silla. Silla king Pŏphŭng (r. 514–40) sent the daughter of the noble Pijobu to marry Tae Kaya king Inoe (dates unknown). The T'aksun state in Ch'angwŏn grew suspicious of Tae Kaya's marriage alliance with Silla and demanded that Tae Kaya break it off. After and although Tae Kaya responded that it intended to keep the marriage pact with Silla, Silla moved to censure T'aksun by taking five Kaya strongholds and annexing the T'akkit'an state in Ch'angnyŏng county. Silla went on to incorporate the Kŭmgwan state in Kimhae in 532. Silla gave the royal descendants of Kŭmgwan Kaya noble true-bone status and the former king Kim Kuhae was awarded his hereditary domain as a prebendal fief. In 531 Paekche took advantage of divisions in Kaya and erected a fortress in Kuryemora, stationed troops in the northern part of the T'aksun state and exerted influence over the Alla state in Haman. The king of T'aksun secretly requested Silla forces to drive Paekche out, and Silla succeeded in expelling the Paekche soldiers positioned at Kurye Mountain Fortress in 544.

The Kaya confederacy bifurcated along north–south lines in the middle of the sixth century following the Tae Kaya state in Koryŏng and the Alla state in Haman. Paekche held two conferences in their capital, Sabi, in 541 and 544, but both broke down because of differences of opinion. The Alla state grew suspicious of Paekche's intentions and requested that Koguryŏ attack it. Nevertheless, Paekche king Sŏng assumed the role of the great lord of the alliance between Paekche, Kaya and Wa and exerted influence over the latter two. Paekche and Silla had been allies against Koguryŏ since 433, and jointly conquered the Han river basin in 551. Although Paekche sought to mobilize Kaya and Wa forces to attack Silla, Silla struck first in 553, seizing the lower reaches of the Han river basin near present-day Seoul. Paekche king Sŏng coordinated an alliance to counterattack, supplemented by 2,000 Kaya soldiers and 1,000 Wa troops, but he was killed in an ambush and the allied initiative disintegrated. In the aftermath of this debacle, Silla openly annexed as much of the Kaya confederation as it could, integrating Alla in 560 and conquering Tae Kaya in 562 in a surprise attack of 5,000 mounted warriors led by the Silla *hwarang* ('flower boy') Sadaham. The remaining states in the Kaya confederacy surrendered to Silla after the fall of Tae Kaya.

Kaya's Intermediary Diplomacy with Paekche and Yamato Wa

Japanese Kokugaku ('national learning') scholars of the Edo period (1603–1868), extrapolating from the *Record of Ancient Matters* (*Kojiki*) and *Chronicles of Japan* (*Nihon shōki*), asserted that the ancient empress Jingū (traditionally 169–269) made a successful expedition against Silla and established a governmental bureau called the 'Mimana Nihonfu' ('Japanese Office in Imna'). During the colonial period (1910–45), the existence of the Mimana Nihonfu was used to justify Japanese colonial intentions and practices, such as harsh modernization policies. Since the demise of the imperial Japanese state, scholars in both Korea and Japan have questioned the role and function of the Mimana Nihonfu. Nevertheless, there was a complex relationship between the Kaya confederacy and the Wa polities of ancient Japan.

From the second half of the fourth century to the first half of the sixth, relations and trade between Kaya and Wa centred on the Kaya confederacy's importing Wa military power in exchange for sending iron and skilled craftsmen to the Japanese islands. Prior to the first half of the sixth century, Korean–Japanese trade followed the model of Paekche–Kaya–Kyūshū Wa–Yamato Wa. Once Paekche subjugated the eastern part of the Honam region in the early sixth century, it started to have direct exchange with the Japanese islands, particularly the Yamato Wa. Silla's marriage alliance with Tae Kaya in 522 upset Paekche's ambitions. Frustrated by being denied trade benefits, the Kyūshū Wa allied with Silla and

Kaya and, despite being suppressed by the Yamato Wa, disrupted trade between Paekche and the Yamato Wa.

Starting in 531, Paekche exerted influence over Alla, the leading state in the southern branch of the Kaya confederacy. Paekche sought to institute a structure to secure trade more directly with Yamato Wa through a route passing through the present-day Masan and Ch'angwŏn area. Under the influence of Paekche, Alla used its prime location to establish a trade agency between Paekche and Wa. In this context, the so-called 'Mimana Nihonfu' was more

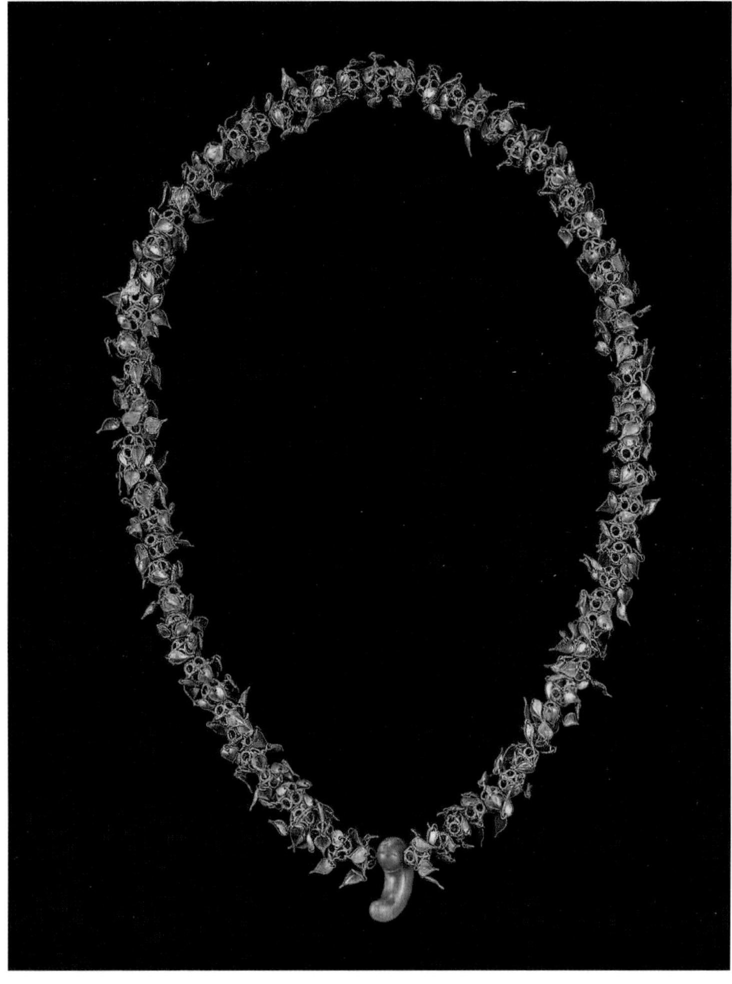

Gold necklace with comma-shaped jade jewel, Silla, 5th century CE.

precisely the Lodging for Wa Officials in Alla and was instituted to fit the designs of Paekche and the needs of Alla. When Silla drove the Paekche forces out of Kurye Mountain Fortress in 544, Alla was able to reorganize the Lodging for Wa Officials to suit its own prerogatives. A close reading of the evidence in the *Chronicles of Japan* demonstrates that the officials of the Lodging for Wa Officials in Alla did not have a direct relationship with the Yamato government. They were either Wa natives or people of Wa lineage who had resided on the Korean peninsula for a long time. They participated in debates in the Kaya confederacy and, because of their language abilities, they played a seminal role in establishing diplomatic relations between the Kaya confederacy and the various Wa polities. Thus the Lodging for Wa Officials in Alla functioned more like a government bureau for special foreign affairs. In the 540s it functioned quasi-independently, but by the 550s the Lodging was again briefly under the influence of Paekche as both Kaya and Paekche scrambled to respond to Silla's conquests. After Silla routed the allied forces of Paekche, Kaya and Wa at the Battle of Kwansan Fortress in 554, Paekche-led diplomacy with Wa was halted for a time and the Lodging for Wa Officials ceased to function.

Early Silla

Protected by the T'aebaek and Sobaek mountain ranges to the north and northwest and nestled in the fertile Kyŏngju plain, Silla emerged as the dominant force among the twelve Chinhan polities during the fourth century. Traditional narratives assert that the state was originally called Sŏrabŏl and later Saro, both of which appear to be cognate to the modern Korean word for 'capital' – commonly known in English as 'Seoul'. Silla was originally a tribal state centred on the present-day environs of Kyŏngju. It was divided into six regions, each of which was headed by a chief (*kanji*). These chiefs met regularly in a council of nobles (*hwabaek*) headed by the Silla king as a first among equals. The royal titles of kings in the 'Annals of Silla' in the *History of the Three Kingdoms* describe an evolution in Silla's kingship in the ancient period: *kŏsŏgan* ('great khan'), *ch'ach'aung* ('shaman [lord]'), *isagŭm* ('successor prince') and *maripkan* ('elevated chieftain'). Although the *History of the Three Kingdoms* says that Silla kings held the title *maripkan* beginning in the early fifth century with King Nulchi (traditionally r. 417–58), the dynastic chronology in *Memorabilia of the Three Kingdoms* first uses the title with Naemul (traditionally r. 356–402).

Extant inscriptions on stone monuments erected by Koguryŏ and Silla during the late fifth and the sixth centuries, however, use the term *maegŭm* or *maegŭmwang* to refer to Silla's 'king of state'. Although most Korean scholars hold the position that *maegŭmwang* is cognate with *maripkan*, the *History of the Three Kingdoms* reports that Silla king Chijŭng (r. 500–514) adopted the sinitic title *wang* ('king') in the tenth lunar month of 503. Nevertheless, Silla king Pŏphŭng (r. 514–40) is still referred to as a *maegŭmwang* in the Pongp'yŏng Stele discovered in Ulchin county, which dates to 524. The prerogatives and hereditary privileges of the nobility were represented on the council of nobles by a secondary king called a *kalmunwang*. Anecdotes relate that the decisions made by the council of nobles needed to be unanimous. The Silla king resided in the T'ak region and the *kalmunwang* in the Sat'ak region. As Silla grew and expanded, particularly in the sixth century, so did the size of the council of nobles.

Due to its location in the southeastern sector of the Korean peninsula, Silla was initially comparatively backward and sluggish in its development in comparison to Koguryŏ and Paekche, which had more direct contact with Chinese states during the Northern and Southern Dynasties period (420–589). In addition, Silla was in a subordinate, protectorate relationship with Koguryŏ in the late fourth and early fifth centuries. Early on this served Silla well because Koguryŏ forces saved Silla when it was overrun in a concerted invasion by Paekche, Kaya and Wa in 400, after suffering constant foreign incursions since 391. Koguryŏ military advisers were posted to Silla during the fifth century, and Silla likely adopted and adapted its early approach to government offices and titles in its capital-rank system from Koguryŏ. In this context, members of the Silla royal family served as hostages to their powerful northern neighbour. For example, Silsŏng (r. 402–17), the son of a high-ranking noble, was sent as a hostage to Koguryŏ in 393 and

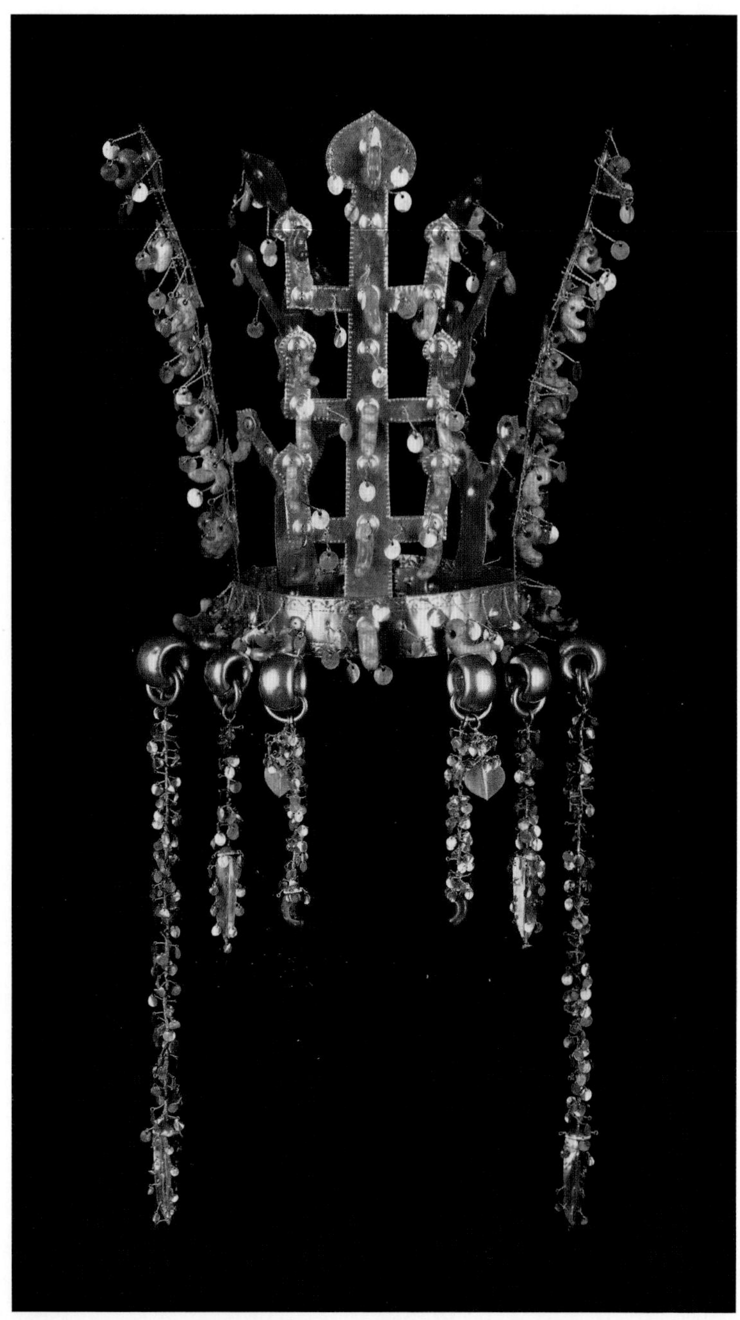

Silla gold crown, Tomb of the Gold Crown, Kyŏngju, second half of the 5th century CE.

Silla conical gilt-bronze crown, Tomb of the Gold Crown, Kyŏngju, 5th century CE.

ascended the throne as a *maripkan* in 402 after returning from service. Silla also sent hostages to the early Japanese Wa polity; the most famous and last case being that of the Silla prince Misahŭn (d. 433), who in 418 (after sixteen years in Wa) was rescued by a loyal Silla retainer who stayed behind to perish to ensure the prince's safe return to his homeland.

Impressive gold crowns and elaborate horse trappings have been excavated from several Silla tombs dated from the late fourth to the early sixth centuries. These grave goods are typically presented as evidence supporting the advancement of the Silla king's position vis-à-vis the hereditary nobility. Silla's gold crowns are so spectacular that they have become emblematic of Silla culture.

Silla crowns come in two types: 'conical caps' (*mogwan*) and 'headband crowns' (*taegwan*). Silla headgear depicted in textual and material culture sources, such as small clay figures interred in tombs, is always the conical-cap style; there are no references to or images of the headband crown. The conical-cap crown (see p. 83) comprises a birchbark frame covered with fabric, and the kind of metal used to adorn it depended on the rank of its wearer; such headgear for members of the royal family and nobility was made from fine silk and precious metals. The cap was worn over the topknot and secured by two hanging straps tied below the chin. Usually found in tombs of males, it is believed to represent secular authority. An example excavated from the southern mound of the Great Tomb of Hwangnam (*Hwangnam taech'ong*) comprises a wing-shaped ornament along with the cap structure. Similar kinds of wing-shaped ornaments were found in the Heavenly Horse Tomb (*Ch'ŏnmach'ong*) and the Gold Crown Tomb (*Kŭmgwanch'ong*). Silla's wing-shaped ornament (see p. 102) probably evolved from

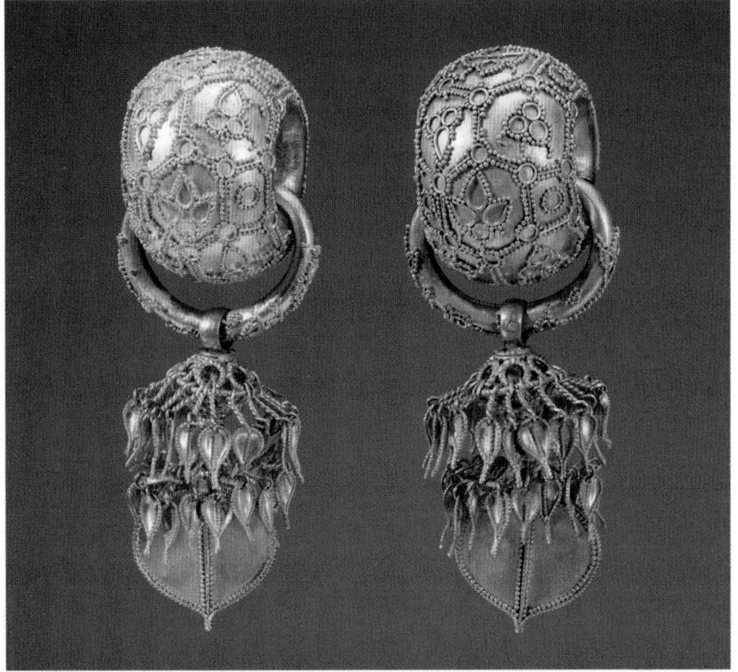

Silla gold earrings, Tomb of the Husband and Wife, Kyŏngju, mid-6th century CE.

the feather-shaped ornaments of the headgear of Koguryŏ nobles and the flower-shaped ornaments of Paekche aristocrats.

The headband crown (see p. 82) comprises a circular headband usually with vertical ornaments arranged pointing upward and downward. The headband and ornaments are made from thin sheets of gold attached by means of a piece of fabric to the inner side of the headband for greater comfort. Deceased members of Silla's royal family, both male and female, were interred wearing the headband crown. Due to their fragile structure, some scholars have advanced the position that these spectacular crowns were primarily grave goods. Others assert that such crowns served a ceremonial or ritual purpose. Upward-facing ornaments appear shaped like deer antlers or trees adorned with small bangles and comma-shaped jade pieces (*kogok* in Korean, *magatama* in Japanese), and usually two downward-hanging ornaments are similar to large earrings with pendant bangles. Because the third-century *Monograph on the Three Kingdoms* describes a sacred tree site (*sodo*) among the Three Han tribes as a large tree hung with drums and bells, some scholars think that the crown symbolized the king's role as a shamanic mediator between heaven and earth. The Silla court appears to have distributed crowns to nobles and chiefs in outlying areas as a means of rewarding subordinates with prestige goods to consolidate power. Although headband crowns became more lavish with time, with tiers or branches increasing from three to four, the function of these crowns as symbols of royal authority and spiritual power eventually declined. After the adoption of Buddhism in the sixth century, the relevance of headband crowns waned, and, by the first half of the seventh century, Silla crowns were made more economically with copper sheets. There is much scholarly debate on the significance of the change from exquisite gold to inexpensive copper crowns. Does it manifest the deterioration of the Silla king's theocratic importance, the replacement of indigenous religious mores with cosmopolitan Buddhist piety and patronage, or the growing relevance of Confucian-oriented frugality?

The Rise of Kingship in Silla

When King Chijŭng ascended the Silla throne in 500, he initiated a process that transformed Silla from arguably the most backward of the Korean states to the dominant power on the peninsula. Early in his reign, in 502, he reportedly outlawed the funerary practice of burying living attendants with deceased royalty; he renamed the country 'Silla' and adopted the Sinitic title for 'king' (*wang* in Korean and Chinese) in 503; he organized the prefectures, commanderies and districts of his domain in 505; and he built fortresses and strongholds throughout Silla territory. His son and successor King Pŏphŭng promulgated criminal and administrative codes in 520, established the position of the senior grandee (*sangdaedŭng*) in 531 to head the council of nobles, absorbed the Kŭmgwan Kaya state in 532, and officially promoted Buddhism as a state religion by beginning work on Hŭngnyun Monastery in 535. In the second half of the twentieth century, scholars understood the institution of the office of senior grandee as a necessary power-sharing concession to Silla nobles in exchange for agreement by the council of nobles to patronize Buddhism. However, more recent scholarship has shown that because the secondary king, the *kalmunwang*, already represented the hereditary nobility on the council of nobles, actually the opposite was the case: the senior grandee represented royal authority and enabled Silla kings to attain a more transcendent position vis-à-vis the nobility.

Silla king Chinhŭng (r. 540–76) was the son of Pŏphŭng's brother, the *kalmunwang* Ipchong. He ascended the throne at the tender age of seven and, upon reaching the age of majority, he embarked on a period of expansion unparalleled in earlier Silla history. In concert with Paekche, he initially conquered the upper reaches of the Han river basin in 551, and later snatched the lower reaches of the Han river basin from Paekche in 553. He oversaw the conquest of Tae Kaya in 562, the assimilation of the remaining states of the Kaya confederation soon thereafter, and the expansion of Silla's borders northward into Koguryŏ territory. He erected four stone monuments commemorating his conquests and the new boundaries of Silla: the stele at Mount Pukhan, likely erected

Detail of Silla envoy (centre) in *Liang Tribute Register* (*Wanghuitu*), *c.* 552–4 CE, ink on paper scroll.

around 568, celebrates Silla's conquest of the prized region surrounding present-day Seoul; the stele at Ch'angnyŏng in 561 remembers a gathering of capital-based nobles and provincial elites after Silla secured complete control of the Naktong river basin; and the steles at Hwangch'o Pass and Maun Pass, likely erected in 568, articulate Silla's relationship with the native peoples of the subjugated regions in the north, some of whom were formerly Koguryŏ subjects. These steles advance the policies of 'rule by force' and 'rule by virtue', and, more importantly, warned his new subjects of swift retribution for subversive behaviour. King Chinhŭng also instituted the *hwarang* order, which will be discussed in more detail in Chapter Four. In 566 Chinhŭng began work on Hwangnyongsa (August Dragon Monastery), a massive monastic complex that functioned as the locus of Buddhist rituals for the protection of the state and the promotion of the royal family. Although Silla's conquest of the Han river basin enabled more direct and frequent access to Chinese states, it engendered imbalance in interstate relations with Paekche and Koguryŏ, leading to a fully fledged diplomatic crisis during the reigns of King Chinp'yŏng (r. 579–632) and queens Sŏndŏk (r. 632–47) and Chindŏk (r. 647–54).

Early Silla society was governed by the bone-rank system (*kolp'umje*), a system of two bone ranks and, putatively, six head ranks. Holy bone (*sŏnggol*) was the highest bone rank, and it was possessed solely by members of the Silla royal family. Holy-bone status was transmitted to a ruler jointly from both father and mother, so, like many ruling dynasties in the premodern world, the

Stele of the inspection of Silla king Chinhŭng on Mt Pukhan, *c.* 568 CE.

Silla royal family practised endogamy. This was likely a contributing factor to holy-bone rulers' dying out in the mid-seventh century following the reigns of queens Sŏndŏk and Chindŏk. The holy-bone royalty was followed by the true-bone (*chin'gol*) nobility. True-bone nobles began as closely related capital-based elites and were typically lesser members of the Silla royal family, which adopted the surname Kim during the second half of the sixth century. Some Kaya nobles, such as the ruling family of Kŭmgwan Kaya in Kimhae that submitted to Silla rule in 532, were also awarded true-bone status. This was the family of the famous Silla general Kim Yusin. Although the two families were closely entwined during the seventh century, what later became known as the Kyŏngju Kim descent group was different from the Kimhae Kim descent group. Kim Ch'unch'u (604–661), who provided important service as a statesman during the reigns of Sŏndŏk and Chindŏk, eventually ascended the throne as the first true-bone king of Silla. Although he was a grandson of the holy-bone Silla king Chinji (r. 576–9), his father Yongsu (aka Yongch'un, *c.* 580–after 643) only possessed true-bone status because his mother was not of the royal family. Kim Ch'unch'u married Kim Yusin's younger sister Munhŭi (later Queen Munmyŏng), who also possessed true-bone status. The close bond, secured by marriage ties, between Kim Ch'unch'u and Kim Yusin was a contributing factor in the success and stability of the fledgling true-bone royal family in the turbulent seventh century.

Although the bone-rank system postulates the existence of six head ranks, little is known about persons of head rank five and below because they are not mentioned in surviving materials. Individuals possessing status of head rank six (*yuktup'um*) were probably tribal chiefs integrated into the growing Silla polity at a much earlier stage, as well as members of the vanquished nobilities of Koguryŏ and Paekche. Head-rank six elites were generally disadvantaged in Silla society. Their comparatively low birth status disqualified them from attaining high office and rank in Silla's government. Some attempted to compensate by focusing on what we might call cultural or educational resources. Some men possessing head-rank six status became famous scholar monks, such as Wŏn'gwang (d. *c.* 640) and Wŏnhyo (617–686). Others pursued Confucian learning, studied in China, passed the Chinese civil service examination and/or served in the civil administration in Tang China, such as Sŏl Kyedu (*fl.* 621), Wŏnhyo's son Sŏl Ch'ong (*c.* 660–730) and Ch'oe Ch'iwŏn (857–after 908). Scholars generally theorize that people possessing head ranks five and four were local functionaries and those possessing head ranks three to one were peasants and slaves.

Silla's capital-rank system was closely related to the bone-rank system. Although the *History of the Three Kingdoms* presents a narrative asserting that the fully evolved system of seventeen ranks was originally instituted by the early King Yuri (traditionally r. 24–57 CE), evidence from epigraphy reveals that the system actually developed over the course of the sixth century as Silla expanded and integrated nobles from the Kaya confederation and other subjugated regions. In its fully articulated form, only true-bone nobles could hold ranks 1 to 5, head-rank six elites could advance as far as rank 6, head-rank five persons could only go as far as rank 10, and head-rank four individuals could only rise to rank 11.

During his long reign spanning the late sixth and early seventh centuries, Silla king Chinp'yŏng instituted several Chinese-style offices that helped evolve the central government. More importantly, he sought recognition by the Sui dynasty, which had reunified northern and southern China in 589. He was recognized as 'Senior Commander, Lord of Nangnang (Lelang), King of Silla' in 594 and sent envoys bearing tribute in local products in 596. Although Silla enjoyed relative peace with Paekche and Koguryŏ in the late sixth century, as mentioned in Chapter Two, after Paekche king Mu assumed the throne in 600 he embarked on an ambitious programme to retake strongholds captured by Silla during the preceding fifty years. In addition, worried about incursions from Koguryŏ along its vulnerable northern borders, Chinp'yŏng sent memorials requesting military aid from the Sui emperor in 608 and 611, which precipitated Sui's invasions of Koguryŏ treated in Chapter Two. Silla's relations with Koguryŏ continued to intensify after the demise of the Sui. In 625 Silla sent an envoy bearing tribute to the newly established Tang dynasty, and a missive accusing Koguryŏ of impeding the passage of Silla emissaries. Koguryŏ and

Paekche engaged in regular attempts to conquer strongholds and fortresses held by Silla, which had been captured previously during the reign of Chinhŭng.

The Silla–Tang Alliance and the Conquest of Paekche and Koguryŏ

Because Chinp'yŏng had no male heirs who could inherit the throne, his daughter Tŏngman ascended the throne in 632 as Silla's first reigning queen, Sŏndŏk. She continued to cultivate a close relationship with Tang, was enfeoffed as 'Pillar of State, Lady of Nangnang (Lelang), Queen of Silla' in 635, and sent multiple tribute-bearing missions to Tang, especially late in her reign. In historical narratives, Sŏndŏk is remembered as a wise and sagacious ruler. Late in her reign, in the eleventh month of 646, she made the *ich'an* (rank 2) Pidam the senior grandee, perhaps hoping that he would oversee the passing of the throne to her chosen successor, her cousin Sŭngman, who would eventually rule as Queen Chindŏk. While she lay on her deathbed in the first lunar month of 647, Pidam rose in revolt, declaring that a queen was unfit to rule. The insurgency lasted more than a week, but General Kim Yusin, who commanded the forces loyal to Sŏndŏk, successfully quelled the uprising.

After Chindŏk ascended the throne, she was enfeoffed with the same titles as Sŏndŏk and dispatched three separate missions to Tang in 648. That same year she wove on silk a regulated verse poem titled 'Song of Great Peace' ('T'aep'yŏngsong') that she had composed. The poem, comprising twenty lines of five sinographs, extols the virtue and achievements of the Tang dynasty. Kim Ch'unch'u's son Kim Pŏmmin (626–681; King Munmu, r. 661–81) was dispatched to present it to Tang emperor Gaozong (r. 649–83). One of the most important developments in Silla's institutional history occurred in the second lunar month of 651, when Chindŏk renamed the Granary Authority the Chancellery. The Chancellery was charged with the duty of promulgating the ruler's orders. Furthermore, head-rank six elites could serve as the director of this office, suggesting that Silla rulers hoped to utilize talented individuals and, simultaneously, curb the influence of true-bone nobles at court. Although the Chancellery did not replace the decision-making power of the council of nobles, it supported the gradual and calculated attempt by Silla monarchs to assume greater autocratic power.

Silla's third mission to Tang in 648 was led by the true-bone noble and statesman Kim Ch'unch'u. He depicted Silla as a classical tributary state and requested that Silla be allowed to adopt Tang official court dress. He asked to visit the Imperial University, to observe the sacrificial rituals performed for Confucius, and to attend lectures on Confucius' *Analects*. Tang emperor Taizong also bestowed on him copies of the most respected and renowned literary and historiographical writings of the early Tang period – which provided Silla scholars with models to improve their writing in what historical linguists call 'literary Sinitic', the written lingua franca of East Asia at the time. One of the most important achievements of Kim Ch'unch'u's 648 mission to Tang was, at best, a secondary objective of his visit. This was the placement of his third son Munwang in a sinecure position as a leader among the emperor's

Long-necked jar with human and animal figurines, Silla, 5th century CE.

personal bodyguard. In time, many royal sons and close relatives of Silla's power elite travelled to Tang for varying terms of service as what may be styled 'external hostages'. Not only did these young men serve as insurance against betrayal by Silla, but, more importantly, their service provided Silla with added prestige and a sympathetic ear at the Tang court.

Although never stated explicitly, the narrative of the *History of the Three Kingdoms* implies that Kim Ch'unch'u and Kim Yusin were the true architects of the strategy to conquer both Paekche and Koguryŏ with the assistance of Tang. Securing Tang forces for an expedition against Paekche was Ch'unch'u's primary objective in 648. Although he succeeded in having some Tang troops allocated to attack Paekche, Tang emperor Taizong's untimely death in 649 put the invasion plans on hold. Remembered in history as Great King Muyŏl (r. 654–61), Kim Ch'unch'u ascended the Silla throne in 654, and worried about the fate of his country as Silla faced continuing incursions by Paekche. Tang emperor Gaozong, aided by the counsel of Empress Wu Zetian (Wu Zhao, 624–705), who had recently engineered her rise to the position of primary consort in 655, dispatched a large invasion fleet under the command of General Su Dingfang (591–667). He was assisted by Ch'unch'u's son Kim Inmun (629–694), who served for many years as Silla's 'external hostage' and liaison with the Tang court. Ground forces led by Silla general Kim Yusin had to defeat Paekche forces led by General Kyebaek that were stationed in a redoubt at Hwangsan (present-day Yŏnsan in South Ch'ungch'ŏng province) before they could meet up with the Chinese forces led by General Su outside the Paekche capital. Because the Silla troops were late to the rendezvous, Su wanted to behead the Silla military leader, Kim Munyŏng. Infuriated, Kim Yusin brandished a battle axe, vowing that he was willing to fight the Tang before settling the score with Paekche. Su's subordinates encouraged leniency, and the joint Tang–Silla forces charged ahead to the Paekche capital, which surrendered on the eighteenth day of the seventh month of 660.

Although the kingdom of Paekche was destroyed and King Ŭija and his heir apparent Prince Yung were taken to Tang as hostages, remaining Paekche nobles fled to and sought assistance from their allies in Yamato Japan to restore the kingdom. Prince P'ung, who was a hostage at the Yamato court, was declared king of Paekche to create a rallying point. Despite their endeavours, Silla and Tang forces were able to capture important Paekche restorationist strongholds, and they crushed the attempted landing of Yamato naval forces at the Battle of Paek River on the 27th day of the eighth month in 663.

In 661, after the conquest of the Paekche capital, General Su sailed his fleet up the Taedong river and attempted a frontal assault on P'yŏngyang, the Koguryŏ capital, hoping to accomplish the Tang's primary objective of subjugating Koguryŏ in the same season. The Tang emperor ordered the newly enthroned Silla king Munmu to mobilize and lead troops to support the gambit, but Munmu declined because he was in mourning for his deceased father, King Muyŏl (Kim Ch'unch'u). With the final demise of Paekche, the Tang and Silla forces had access to Koguryŏ's soft underbelly without fear of fighting Paekche simultaneously on a southern front. Nevertheless, the allies were not able to make any sustainable progress in the conquest of Koguryŏ until after the death of the hegemon Yŏn Kaesomun in 665. After he had murdered the Koguryŏ king and usurped control of the court for more than twenty years, Yŏn's passing unleashed a bitter power struggle between his sons and his younger brother. His eldest son, Yŏn Namsaeng, was exiled through an intrigue engineered by his second son, Yŏn Namgŏn. Namsaeng fled to Kungnaesŏng, the old Koguryŏ capital, and submitted to Tang. At roughly the same time, Yŏn Kaesomun's younger brother, Yŏn Chŏngt'o, surrendered to Silla. Both provided the intelligence necessary for the allied Tang and Silla forces to overcome Koguryŏ's extensive defences, and Koguryŏ finally capitulated in 668. Resistance to incorporation into the Tang empire emerged by way of a former mid-ranking official named Kŏmmojam (d. 670). Although he swore allegiance to Ansŭng, an 'illegitimate' son of King Pojang (r. 642–68) – that is, a son born by a concubine rather than his primary consort – and resisted Tang attempts to mop up the restorationist forces, in the end Kŏmmojam was eliminated on Ansŭng's orders. Soon thereafter, Ansŭng submitted to Silla and was put to use by the Silla court to advance its own objectives.

Although Silla had succeeded in preserving itself and destroying its powerful neighbours Paekche and Koguryŏ through the deft use of the mighty Chinese ally, the Tang, it had merely traded one form of insecurity for another. The Tang forces did not pack up and leave the Paekche region, but instead seemed to be forming administrative organs to incorporate it into the Tang empire. Whatever understanding Kim Ch'unch'u had reached with Tang emperor Taizong regarding the map of the post-war Korean peninsula did not translate to his son Gaozong and the ambitious Empress Wu. The period of Greater Silla continues this thread of the historical narrative, with Silla's skilful use of diplomacy, guerrilla warfare, tribute bearing and fortuitous circumstances enabling it to become the dominant power on the peninsula until the late ninth century.

FOUR
Religion and Culture in the Early Three Kingdoms

Life in the Three Kingdoms period was delimited by one's social status and the cultural practices of each individual kingdom, including religious beliefs and rituals. Early Chinese observers, such as official emissaries and merchants, as well as literate Koreans of later periods, recognized, recorded and postulated both similarities and differences in the lifestyles and outlooks of the early Korean peoples. Due to the preponderance of cultural resemblances, Chinese writers originally coined the inclusive geographical term 'Three Kingdoms East of the Sea' (*haedong samguk*) to refer to the countries that would eventually coalesce into the Korean people. By the late seventh century, the term *haedong* became used as a general designation for the Korean peninsula, specifically the kingdom of Silla. Just as the early Germanic world of Northern Europe was shaped by its encounter with Roman culture and the writings of classical and early medieval Roman authors, the Korean peoples' views of themselves were, from the outset, shaped by Sinitic influences ranging from the use of sinographs ('Chinese characters') in the representation of early forms of the Korean language, and the adoption of large amounts of Chinese vocabulary, to the general approbation enjoyed by Chinese cosmological beliefs, such as the four heraldic animals (that is, the deities of the four directions) and the twelve earthly deities (the animals of the Chinese zodiac). In short, participation in a shared East Asian or Sinitic culture constantly inspired and informed the Korean people and their images of the past until the twentieth century.

The Modes of Ancient Korean Religion

Western scholars have employed several broadly inclusive academic terms to describe religion in early Korea: animism, totemism, shamanism and paganism. Animism is defined as the belief that plants, animals, inanimate objects and natural phenomena are imbued with spiritual essence and can interact with the material world. Totemism is a system of belief in which groups or tribes of humans are believed to have kinship or a mystical relationship with a spirit being, such as a particular type of animal or plant. Shamanism is popularly defined as belief in an unseen world of gods, ghosts, demons and ancestral spirits responsive only to 'shamans'. Shamans, in turn, are defined as religious specialists or spirit mediums who use magic and ritual to cure the sick, divine the hidden and control events. In premodern Korea, shamans in the northern regions are thought to have engaged with the spirit world via possession brought about by ecstatic dancing leading to trance, while those in the south communicated with the spirits via hereditary dances and rituals passed down in shaman families. 'Paganism' is a general Western term used to describe pre-Christian beliefs of ordinary people. It can include belief in gods, ghosts, spirits, nature worship, fertility rituals and other magico-religious practices emphasizing the relationship between humans and nature. Aspects of all of these terms can be found in early Korean religious practices.

Instead of attempting to advance one term, I will here summarize ancient Korean religion as consisting of four aspects or modes: (1) the worship of entities and objects worthy of veneration, (2) the mythology of founder kings, (3) calendrical rituals and (4) the activities of shamans. The peoples of Northeast Asia, including the tribal peoples who would coalesce into the Korean nation, worshipped an assortment of deities, animals, natural wonders and heavenly bodies, such as trees, wells and springs, tigers and dragons. Chinese accounts dating to the third century report that the people of Koguryŏ worshipped ghosts and spirits, the gods of soil and grain, and 'numinous stars' (alluding to the Sinitic deity 'Lord Millet'). Tang historians of the seventh century asserted that although Buddhism was practised

Chŏmsŏngdae Observatory, Wŏlsŏng, Kyŏngju, constructed during the reign of Queen Sŏndŏk (632–47).

in Koguryŏ, its people still performed 'licentious religious services', which for the Chinese meant the propitiation of indigenous spirits (of rivers, lakes, gorges and so on) by means of blood sacrifices and alcoholic offerings. Chinese writers of the tenth century stated that the Koguryŏ people worshipped the sun god, the gods of the khans and the spirit of Kija (Jizi in Chinese), an ancient lord of the Chinese Shang dynasty who was enfeoffed as ruler of the ancient Korean state of Chosŏn in the eleventh century BCE. The peoples of the Three Han tribes also worshipped sundry deities. The Pyŏnhan people, ancestors to the Kaya confederacy, are all said to have had images of the kitchen god on the west side of their doors. Chinese records report that Paekche people regularly worshipped heaven and the spirits of the five thearchs, which likely referred to the five planets: Jupiter, Mars, Saturn, Venus and Mercury. Both of these cases indicate the rising acceptance of Chinese culture, perhaps due to migration and mercantile activities.

Although Chinese historians of the early seventh century intimate that Silla beliefs were similar to those of Koguryŏ and Paekche, they indicate that Silla people worshipped the sun god and the moon god on the first day of each lunar month. Chinese historians of the eleventh century report that mountain spirits were worshipped regularly besides once-yearly veneration of the deities of the sun and moon. The *History of the Three Kingdoms* alludes to an initial system of three mountains in the Kyŏngju plain in early Silla times: Naeryŏk (aka Naerim), Korhwa and Hyŏllye, corresponding to Mount Nang in the east, Mount Kŭmgang in the north and Mount Ori in the southwest. Paekche also seems to have had a system of three mountains in the environs of their final walled capital, Sabi (*c.* 538–660): Mount Paek, Mount O and Mount Pu were the residences of Paekche deities who purportedly flew between them at will.

Chapter One briefly introduced the legends of the founders of the early Korean kingdoms. Chinese dynastic histories of the seventh century report that Koguryŏ's royal cult of the ancestors was venerated at an ancestral temple and that other ancestral

Paekche clay brick with dragon design, Puyŏ, 6th century.

deities were worshipped in ancestral halls. These same texts report that Paekche people offered sacrifices to their founder, Kut'ae, in ancestral halls four times each year, suggesting seasonal offerings. Although the *History of the Three Kingdoms* claims that Pak Hyŏkkŏse was worshipped in each of the four seasons in a 'temple to the first founder', Silla epigraphy and Chinese texts refer only to an unnamed founder king known as the 'Grand Ancestor' from the seventh through ninth centuries. Silla rulers also erected a spirit palace in either 487 or 502, at the place where Pak Hyŏkkŏse putatively descended to earth (Najŏng in Yangsan), as a place to offer sacrifices to the ancestor. The remains of an octagonal wooden structure were discovered through excavation of the site, although the building likely dates from the seventh century or later. Silla kings offered sacrifices at the spirit palace until the end of the dynasty, typically in concert with granting amnesty to prisoners. This suggests a kind of regular ritual festival that could be invoked to ward against calamities and natural disasters, such as famines and pestilence.

Because the early Korean peoples were agrarian, calendrical festivals were vitally important to the cycles of daily life throughout a year. The *Monograph on the Three Kingdoms* briefly describes the 'welcoming drums' ritual of the Puyŏ people who 'sacrifice to heaven using the correct month of Yin (Shang dynasty)' and that they assemble to 'eat and drink, dance and sing for days on end'. The same Chinese text refers to the 'dancing to heaven' festival of the Ye people, held in the tenth lunar month. Along with offering service to heaven, they drank, sang and danced night and day. The calendrical ritual ascribed to the Han tribes of the south presents the most detail:

> In the fifth month when the sowing is finished, they always sacrifice to their ghosts and spirits. Gathering in groups, they sing and dance and they drink wine day and night without ceasing. In their dancing, several tens of men get up together and form a line; looking upward and downward as they stomp the ground, they move hands and feet in concert with a rhythm that is similar to our bell-clapper dance. When the farm work

> is finished in the tenth month, they do the same sort of thing again. They have faith in ghosts and spirits. In each town one man is appointed master of ceremonies for worship of the spirit(s) of heaven, whom they call the 'lord of heaven'. Moreover, each commune has a separate town, which they call *sodo*. Here they set up a great tree, from which they hang bells and drums for serving the ghosts and spirits. All manner of refugees who enter there are exempt from extradition. They have a fondness for brigandage. The significance of their setting up *sodo* is similar to that of our *Buddhastūpas* [Buddhist pagodas], but there are differences to the good and evil they attribute to what they do.[7]

A Chinese history compiled in the seventh century reports that Mahan, which came before Paekche, offered sacrifices to ghosts and spirits in the fifth and tenth months, and that that under the jurisdiction of the 'lord of heaven' people worshipped the spirits of heaven in their villages. Other tribal peoples of Northeast Asia also used drums and wine in their offerings to heaven, such as the Xiongnu (Huns) and the Tuoba (Tabgach) Xianbei who founded the Northern Wei (386–534). Although some scholars assert that the previously mentioned 'lord of heaven' was a shaman and that shamans administered these calendrical rituals, the Chinese texts do not use either of the standard Chinese terms for male and female shamans to describe the lord of heaven. My reading of the passage is that a locally prominent man was provisionally and temporarily appointed to be the supervisor of the village ritual invoking success and gratitude for the planting and harvesting of the grain crops. The lord of heaven was not the only person able to venerate the ghosts and spirits at the *sodo*, but merely superintended and regulated the worship therein.

Seventh-century Chinese histories state that Koguryŏ gathered its people together for a great assembly in the tenth lunar month each year in which Tongmyŏng, the founder king, was honoured and offerings to heaven could be made. Chinese records from the seventh and tenth centuries also relate that Silla held an important ritual associated with the harvest on the fifteenth day of the eighth lunar month and that the mountain spirit or mountain spirits were venerated. As Chinese culture permeated Silla, they also held celebratory rituals on the first day of the first lunar month and worshipped the sun and the moon on the ninth day of the ninth lunar month.

The *History of the Three Kingdoms* and the *Memorabilia of the Three Kingdoms* refer to shamans a total of eleven times. The five references to shamans active in Koguryŏ depict them in roles similar to shamans today: spirit mediumship, exorcism and the pacification of vengeful spirits, and providing assistance to kings in the performance of ancestral rituals. The two accounts dealing with Paekche portray the shaman in a divinatory role, solving a riddle written on the back of a turtle that foretells the demise of the kingdom and explaining why a cow was born with one head and two bodies. The four cases associated with Silla provide the

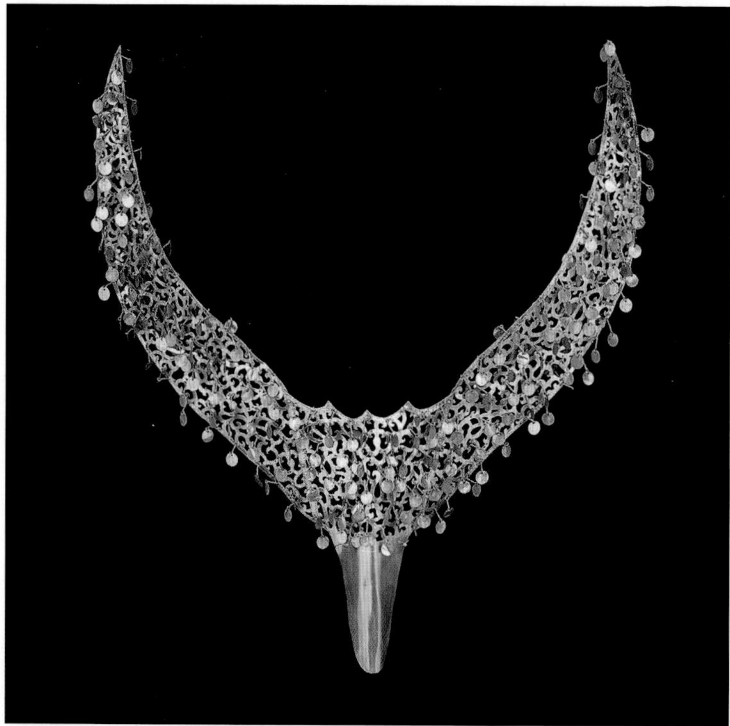

Winged-shaped crown ornament, Silla, Tomb of the Heavenly Horse, Kyŏngju, 6th century CE.

strongest literary evidence both of the purported elevated status of shamans in early Silla and of ambivalence regarding shamans' skills after the arrival of Buddhist monks who rivalled shamans as spiritual healers. In an interlinear note, Kim Pusik reports that Silla historian Kim Taemun (*fl.* 704) glossed the early regal title *ch'ach'aung* or *chach'ung* as meaning 'shaman' (*mu* in Korean). The fact that shamans are not mentioned in accounts of the early Korean states in Chinese historiography suggests that the early Koreans did not need to rely on such specialists and, in many cases, nobles and other social elites typically venerated the spirits on their own authority. Shamans were likely consulted when problems with spirits could not be resolved in other ways.

Social Status and Society in the Three Kingdoms

Although little is known regarding most of the early Korean kingdoms, with the exception of Silla, birth status and hereditary privilege played an important role in the construction of social stratification. In Koguryŏ, archaeological evidence and remaining literary accounts suggest that there was a general distinction between an aristocracy and a lower stratum called the 'lower households' (*haho*). From the first century BCE to the third century CE, Koguryŏ was centred on five tribes: Sono, Yŏnno, Kwanno, Chŏllo and Kyeru. The Sono tribe (probably the Piryang tribe of the Koguryŏ annals in the *History of the Three Kingdoms*) was replaced by the Kyeru tribe as the ruling descent group in the first century CE. As Koguryŏ continued to grow, although the five tribes were still important, other tribal groups joined the ruling elite, especially after the succession dispute in the year 200 and after the capital moved to Kungnaesŏng (modern Ji'an) in the fourth century. The Koguryŏ aristocracy was centred, of course, on the royal family and the other privileged descent groups from which Koguryŏ kings chose their queens. Some rank titles were possessed only by scions of honoured clans. For instance, the royal Ko family was of the Kyeru lineage, but *kuch'uga*, the highest honorary title in Koguryŏ, could be possessed only by someone of the former royal family of the Sono lineage and of the Myŏngnim family of the Yŏnna

(Chŏllo) lineage that supplied royal consorts. Several other social strata appear to have existed beneath this upper crust, and marriage between individuals of different social status appears to have been forbidden.

Similar to Koguryŏ, Paekche's leadership was concentrated around several prominent descent groups. Although the *History of the Sui Dynasty* (*Sui shu*) mentions eight such families, the Chin, Hae, Sa (Sat'aek), Yŏn, Hyŏp, Kuk, Mok and Paek, 90 per cent of the references to non-royal people in the Paekche annals in the *History of the Three Kingdoms* belong to the first four. The highest government offices, however, were dominated by the royal Puyŏ clan and the Chin and Hae families that supplied most of the known Paekche queens. Individuals who served in the leading administrative positions outside the capital, such as the short-lived *tamno* system of 22 fiefs, were drawn exclusively from the royal family. Thus the royal family of Paekche appears to have enjoyed the pre-eminent position in Paekche society. Small administrative councils, the purpose of which was to advise the king and elect chief ministers to lead the officialdom, probably comprised elites from a select group of aristocratic families. The three tiers of coloured robes in Paekche's sixteen-level officialdom also probably reflected the realities of Paekche's social structure.

The Silla annals in the *History of the Three Kingdoms* assert that Silla (Sŏnabŏl, Sŏrabŏl) was founded in 57 BCE by the golden boy Hyŏkkŏse who was given the surname Pak. It was centred on six villages in what is now the Kyŏngju basin, and in 32 CE the *isagŭm* Yuri (traditionally r. 24–57) assigned new names to each of the six villages, and surnames to people living in each village. The Silla annals then craft a narrative that rule of Silla passed between three royal families, Pak, Sok and Kim, until the Kim descent group kept control of the throne from the time of the *isagŭm* Mich'u (traditionally r. 262–84). These six villages evolved into the six regions of Silla: T'akpu (Yangbu), Sat'akpu (Saryangbu), Chŏmnyangbu (Moryangbu), Ponp'ibu, Han'gibu and Sŭppibu. However, there is no corroborative evidence from early epigraphy that any Silla nobles residing in these possessed or used surnames until the second half of the sixth century. Silla elites likely did not adopt

Stele of Paekche nobleman Sat'aek Chijŏk, Puyŏ, 654 CE, stone.

Chinese-style surnames until after the conquest of the Han river basin and the Kaya confederacy, when contact with Chinese states became more regular, because they needed to show that they possessed some of the basic trappings of civilized states. Surnames do not appear in Silla epigraphy until the late seventh century, after the unification wars. Nobles belonging to what we now refer to as the Kyŏngju Kim descent group dominated the highest positions in government. Because the Silla royal house typically practised endogamy, some Silla queens were likely surnamed Pak retroactively to avoid Chinese accusations of improper behaviour as Silla adopted Sinitic culture and attempted to portray itself as a civilized Confucian state. Chinese materials from the seventh and eighth centuries recognize Kim as Silla's only royal surname and Pak as a surname possessed by social elites. The bone-rank and capital-rank systems, briefly introduced in Chapter Three, most likely developed in the sixth century and the strictures of the system enabled Silla society to absorb and subordinate elites from subjugated settlements and polities.

Koguryŏ initially established a court-rank system comprising ten levels from the late second century to the third. By the fourth century, this was expanded to a system of twelve levels. Following the model established by Koguryŏ, Paekche had developed a sixteen-level court-rank system by the mid-sixth century at the latest. Silla's court-rank system evolved over the course of the sixth century and achieved its final seventeen-level form in the second half of the sixth century. The similarities between the three systems are striking enough that both the Paekche and Silla systems, as well

Tile with floral medallion and dragon design, Silla, late 7th century CE.

as early Japan's twelve-rank system established by Suikō (r. 593–628) in 603, developed under the influence of Koguryŏ.

Capital-Rank Systems of the Three Kingdoms

Koguryŏ's Twelve Ranks
1. taedaero, 2. t'aedaehyŏng, 3. ulchŏl, 4. t'aedaesaja, 5. choŭidudaehyŏng, 6. taesaja, 7. taehyŏng, 8. suwisaja, 9. sosaja, 10. sohyŏng, 11. chehyŏng, 12. sŏnin

Paekche's Sixteen Ranks
1. chwap'yŏng, 2. talsol, 3. ŭnsol, 4. tŏksol, 5. hansol, 6. nasol (purple robes), 7. changdŏk, 8. sidŏk, 9. kodŏk, 10. kyedŏk, 11. taedŏk (scarlet robes), 12. mundŏk, 13. mudŏk, 14. chwagun, 15. chinmu, 16. kŭgu (blue robes)

Silla's Seventeen Ranks
1. ibŏlch'an, 2. ich'ŏkch'an, 3. chapch'an, 4. p'ajinch'an, 5. taeach'an (purple robes), 6. ach'an, 7. ilgilch'an, 8. sach'an, 9. kŭppŏlch'an (scarlet robes), 10. taenama, 11. Nama, 12. taesa(ji), 13. saji, 14. kilsa, 15. taeo(ji), 16. soo(ji), 17. chowi (yellow robes)

The Adoption of Buddhism and the Importation of Sinitic Culture

The *History of the Three Kingdoms* reports that Koguryŏ and Paekche adopted Buddhism as an official state religion in 372 and 384 respectively. Although Buddhist monks from Koguryŏ were reportedly active in Silla territory as early as the time of the *maripkan* Nulchi (r. 417–58) and King Pŏphŭng wanted to promote Buddhism as early as 527–8, work did not start on Silla's first monastery until 535. The reluctance of Silla nobles to accept Buddhism is similar to the case of Yamato Japan, whose elites hesitantly embraced Buddhism in the mid- to late sixth century after its 'official' introduction by Paekche king Sŏng (in 552 or 538). Chinese Buddhist sources suggest that Buddhist monks were active as missionaries in Koguryŏ beginning at least in the early fourth century. Furthermore, Paekche's maritime contacts and diplomacy with southern Chinese dynasties, beginning with the Jin (265–420), suggest that Buddhist proselytizers may have been active in the Paekche long before the late fourth century. Nevertheless, the late fourth century and the first half of the sixth are useful dates for understanding when the early Korean kingdoms were open to more vigorous and consistent contact and cultural exchange with mainland Chinese dynasties. More broadly stated, because they enjoyed a longer history of contact with Chinese states, the Koguryŏ and Paekche kingdoms were more sophisticated and prepared much earlier than Silla to engage in the continuous and robust importation of Sinitic (Chinese) culture.

Contact with the northern and southern Chinese dynasties brought prestige to the Korean kings and their states because various Chinese emperors bestowed honorary titles and other paraphernalia upon them, which functioned as symbols of status in the aristocratic world of medieval Northeast Asia. Although the evidence is sketchy at best, traditional East Asian hip-and-gable roof architecture, the design and manufacturing of roof tiles, the production of ink and paper and so forth were transferred to the Korean kingdoms most likely by skilled craftsmen being sent to the Korean peninsula to train or such skilled people immigrating to the peninsula. Many such individuals were Buddhist monks

Hard clay inkstone, Paekche, Puyŏ, 6th–7th century CE.

because of the importance of sūtra chanting in healing practices and of sūtra copying and other practices in daily devotions.

Literacy in literary Sinitic, the written lingua franca of East Asia, was arguably the most important skill transmitted to the Korean peninsula. Evidence of writing is found in the area of the Lelang commandery (present-day P'yŏngyang) as early as the first century BCE, and individuals possessing this skill probably trickled into the Korean states from that time forward. The oldest extant example of Korean epigraphy is the 'Inscription on the Stele Erected in Honour of King Kwanggaet'o', which was erected in 414 – forty years after the adoption of Buddhism in Koguryŏ. In 608 Silla king Chinp'yŏng turned to the Buddhist monk Wŏn'gwang (d. *c.* 640) to compose a memorial to Sui emperor Yang requesting military aid. Wŏn'gwang's biography in *Further Lives of Eminent Monks* (*Xu gaoseng zhuan*, completed in 649) reports that he initially trained in China as a scholar before converting to Buddhism. That the Silla king did not have other officials sufficiently trained in literary composition shows what a rare skill it was even in the early seventh century.

Although monks and nuns read and chanted Buddhist sūtras, monastics from families wealthy enough to educate their children were likely exposed to mainstream Chinese literature in the formative period of their education. This included such widely read 'Confucian' and 'Daoist' works as the *Analects* of Confucius, the *Mencius*, the *Daode jing*, the *Zhuangzi*, the *Book of Filial Piety* (*Xiao jing*), the *Records of the Grand Historian* (*Shiji*), the five Confucian classics, the early Chinese dynastic histories and so forth. Most ordinary people's knowledge of Buddhism was couched in terms of the basic social morality commonly articulated in 'Confucian' terms, along with promises of this-worldly prosperity and protection tied to attentively practising Buddhist devotions, compassionate service to others and generous patronage of the Buddhist church. All of these behaviours produced wholesome karma, and other pious activities promised the elimination of unwholesome karma, leading to better rebirth. The idea that living beings are caught in a cycle of rebirth and death, that one's quality of life in the present is based on past actions (karma) and that only the

Buddhist teaching can free one from being trapped in this cycle – or promise a more fortuitous rebirth – was conveyed to ordinary people by means of narratives and tales, a few of which will be treated briefly in Chapter Six. The royal families and noble houses of the early Korean states, particularly that of Silla, justified their dominance of society in Buddhist terms.

Most ordinary people lived in thatched-roof huts in the early period, but kings and lords increasingly built impressive hip-and-gable roof structures with ceramic roof tiles with the influx of technology from the East Asian continent. Buddhist monasteries and temples constructed on royal command were likely the most imposing buildings ordinary people would see and be able to visit in their lifetimes. Extant carvings in cave temples in China and rock carvings in Korea suggest that Daoist and Buddhist imagery was combined indiscriminately in religious material culture. In religious Daoism, the veneration of transcendent beings and immortals was widespread, and such figures and accompanying motifs as the Queen Mother of the West's peaches that grant immortality, Penglai (Pongnae in Korean) and the islands of the immortals (see p. 68), and flying immortals, appear along with more standard Buddhist motifs, such as lotus flowers, transformation beings born from lotus flowers, honeysuckle motifs and flame patterns. In this way, although in the modern world we like to imagine Confucianism, Buddhism and Daoism as being distinct and discrete religions, in reality most people, including social elites, did not differentiate strictly between the three. Furthermore, because Buddhists and the Buddhist church in northern China were under attack from time to time by some avid proponents of either Confucianism or Daoism, many educated Buddhists advanced the view that the Three Teachings were harmonious and ultimately the same. This assessment allowed for the preservation and longevity of Buddhism in East Asia, but also, more importantly, transformed East Asian Buddhism itself.

The Cults of Buddhas and Bodhisattvas in Mahāyāna Buddhism

The Buddhism that entered the early Korean kingdoms was a form of Mahāyāna Buddhism that integrated Indian-inspired Buddhist doctrines and the veneration of buddhas and bodhisattvas with mainstream Chinese social mores. Worship of the historical Buddha Śākyamuni (Siddhartha Gautama) is fundamental in most forms of Buddhism. An ideal Buddhist king who promotes the Buddhist teaching is called a *cakravartin*, a 'king who turns the wheel of the dharma'. In sixth-century Silla, King Chinhŭng (r. 540–76) named his sons after two of the four kinds of wheel-turning kings: Tongnyun ('bronze wheel') and Saryun (or Kŭmnyun, 'golden wheel'), showing how Buddhist principles were shaping Silla ideas of kingship. Chinhŭng modelled himself on the ancient Indian king Aśoka (traditionally r. 268–232 BCE) and the more recent Liang emperor Wu (r. 502–49), who distinguished himself as a pious patron of Buddhism. In 566 Chinhŭng founded Hwangnyong Monastery, a massive Buddhist educational and ritual centre, on a site east of the royal palace complex at Wŏlsŏng. He originally planned to build a new palace but desisted after sighting a yellow dragon. Hwangnyong Monastery was continually renovated and enlarged and became the state palladium and locus of Buddhist rituals for the protection of the royal family and the country. Stories were circulated that asserted deep connections between Silla and India. One such story was that a curiously shaped stone behind Hwangnyong Monastery was the actual site where the Buddha Kāśyapa of the previous aeon sat when he obtained enlightenment.

Tongnyun's son eventually came to the throne and ruled as King Chinp'yŏng (r. 579–632). Chinp'yŏng's given name was Paekchŏng (Śuddhodana) and his brothers' names were Paekpan (Śuklodana) and Kukpan (Drotodana), the names of Śākyamuni's father and brothers. His wife's name was Lady Maya, the same as the mother of Śākyamuni. Thus, if Chinp'yŏng had had a son, it would be as if the Buddha had been born in Silla. Chinp'yŏng, however, only had daughters. His daughter Tŏngman (perhaps Guṇāmālādevī) succeeded him and ruled as Queen Sŏndŏk (r. 632–47), and her cousin Sŭngman (Śrīmālādevī), the daughter of Kukpan, ruled as Queen Chindŏk (r. 647–54) after her. Sŭngman corresponds to Śrīmālādevī, the name of a famous Buddhist queen found in Mahāyāna Buddhist literature. Sŏndŏk began work on an enormous nine-storey wooden pagoda at Hwangnyong Monastery in 645. She also identified Mount Nang in the Silla capital as Trāyastriṃśā, the heaven where the 33 gods of the Indian pantheon reside at the top of the *axis mundi*, Mount Sumeru. Sŏndŏk had herself buried on Mount Nang; later, in 679, King Munmu built Sach'ŏnwang Monastery on the site to invoke for Silla the protective power of the Four Heavenly Kings, deities that guard the four directions.

Although the ruling family of Silla imagined themselves as being of the *kṣatriya* (warrior) caste, the royalty and nobility of both Paekche and Silla appear to have invoked the Bodhisattva Maitreya, the future Buddha, under whose eyes the Buddhist faithful will enjoy peace and prosperity unknown in previous times. Features of the cult of Maitreya are found in Koguryŏ, Paekche and Silla, but the limited evidence from Koguryŏ suggests that it more closely followed developments in the northern Chinese dynasties, such as the Later Qin (384–417) and Northern Wei. Buddhist sūtras assert that Maitreya is presently in meditation in Tuṣita Heaven, waiting to descend after all traces of the Buddha Śākyamuni and his teaching have been lost. Buddhists in East Asia understood Tuṣita Heaven to be like a 'pure land' where someone could be reborn and live like a Daoist immortal, transcendent being or sylph. Some early devotees of Maitreya sought to be reborn in Tuṣita Heaven to learn the Buddhist teaching directly from him, and others hoped to be reborn in the distant future when Maitreya would hold three assemblies to teach the Buddhadharma after achieving enlightenment under his bodhi tree, 'dragon-flower tree' (*nāgapuṣpa* in Sanskrit). The royalty and nobility of Paekche and Silla, however, imagined more direct connections with Maitreya: that the bodhisattva would appear personally in the present-day world or that Maitreya would come and go many times in a specifically designated country. None of the traditional narratives preserved in *Memorabilia of the Three Kingdoms* regarding the cult of Maitreya mention rebirth in Tuṣita

Heaven as a stated goal of aspirants before Silla's unification of the Three Kingdoms.

Paekche king Mu (r. 600–641) began work on a massive monastic complex at Iksan (in North Ch'ungch'ŏng province) called Mirŭksa (Maitreya Monastery) in 602. The monastery had three compounds, each comprising a golden hall (a building housing an image of Buddha) and a multistorey pagoda, symbolic of Maitreya's three assemblies. Through the construction, Mu prepared a place for Maitreya to descend in the present and seemed to assert that Maitreya had already come or would come immediately. Numerous images of Maitreya depicted as a handsome young man seated in the pensive style were produced in Silla in the late sixth and early seventh centuries prior to unification. Stories linking Maitreya to the *hwarang* were prevalent in Silla, suggesting that Silla Buddhists believed the *hwarang* to be incarnations of the bodhisattva. The oldest narrative tells of a monk named Chinja (*fl.* 576–9) who supplicated before an image of Maitreya, praying that Maitreya would appear in Silla as a *hwarang*. Following a dream, he encountered a youth who was an incarnation of Maitreya at a mountain monastery in Kongju (in Paekche territory), but he did not realize that the young man was the bodhisattva he sought. A mountain spirit informed him of his mistake, and he remembered that the youth had said that he also was a native of the Silla capital. Chinja returned to Silla and eventually found the youth, named Misi, and made him the leader of the *hwarang* – and he was called the 'Maitreya sylph flower'. Misi led the *hwarang* for seven years and then disappeared. Thus Maitreya is active in the present; he is not waiting for the future establishment of his 'pure land'. Silla nobles also commissioned and buried images of Maitreya (sometimes in tombs of deceased youths) in hopes that sons, emblematic of Maitreya, would be born to them who would protect the kingdom as members of *hwarang* bands.

Pensive bodhisattva, Three Kingdoms period, early 7th century CE, gilt bronze.

Pensive bodhisattva, Maitreya, Silla, late 6th–early 7th century CE, gilt bronze.

The Flower Boys (*Hwarang*) of Silla

The traditional narrative describing the origins of the *hwarang* reports that prior to the mid-sixth century Silla had a youth organization focused on young women, called *wŏnhwa* ('original flowers'), who were selected for their physical beauty. After Chinhŭng came to the throne in 540, two attractive maidens contended for the position of supreme *wŏnhwa*. Each had her own group of male and female followers. Because one of the young women was jealous of the other's accomplishments, she got her drunk and murdered her by bashing her head in with a stone by a river. When word reached the king, he reportedly disbanded the *wŏnhwa* and promised to start the programme again with handsome young men in the leadership role. This intriguing story and other terse passages on the *hwarang* were placed at the end of Chinhŭng's annals in the *History of the Three Kingdoms*, implying that the *hwarang* order came into being sometime during his reign.

In effect, youth in Silla's status-oriented society learned the order of the bone-rank system through participating in the *hwarang* organization. The *hwarang* institution, like the *wŏnhwa* programme before it, probably evolved out of village youth organizations of the early Three Kingdoms period. Prior to the institution of the

Silla mounted nobleman and attendant, Tomb of the Golden Bell, Kyŏngju, 6th century CE, stoneware ritual vessel.

State Academy under King Sinmun (r. 681–92), the *hwarang* taught practical and cultural skills to noble youths and their followers; youths who later became leaders of the state. The *hwarang* order comprised several bands, and each *hwarang* band consisted of a leader, called a *hwarang*, of true-bone status, and ranks of followers (*nangdo*). Buddhist monks functioned as spiritual mentors in some *hwarang* bands. The prime age for *hwarang* training was fifteen to eighteen. In the brief accounts found in the *History of the Three Kingdoms*, Kim Pusik emphasizes individual *hwarang* and *hwarang* bands dedicated to the protection of the state by means of military skills. Blood oaths between members of the band and the sacrifice of one's life for the state are presented as the highest code of conduct. In the narratives preserved in *Memorabilia of the Three Kingdoms*, the monk Iryŏn primarily stresses the cultural accomplishments of the *hwarang*, such as the skills of some in composing *hyangga* (native songs), seeking reclusion in the mountains, and beliefs and practices complementary to those of Buddhists. The polysemous terms *p'ungnyu* and *p'ungwŏl* were borrowed from literary aesthetics in the Sinitic cultural sphere to refer to *hwarang* training. The general sense of these terms is 'aristocratic merrymaking', but in the context of the *hwarang* the terms function as referring to 'the customs and practices of the *hwarang*'.

A famous story found in both the *History of the Three Kingdoms* and the *Memorabilia of the Three Kingdoms* regards the 'five secular precepts' given by the monk Wŏn'gwang to the noble youth Kwisan and his friend Ch'uhang in the early seventh century. They sought teachings to follow from the eminent monk so that they might not be ashamed when in the presence of 'ministers and gentlemen'. Neither Kwisan nor Ch'uhang are referred to as *hwarang* or as members of *hwarang* bands, so Wŏn'gwang's instructions cannot be construed as directly applicable to the *hwarang* institution. Nevertheless, his advice certainly encapsulates the spirit of the age. The five precepts were: (1) serve your lord with fealty (loyalty), (2) serve your parents with filial piety, (3) treat your comrades with good faith, (4) do not retreat in the face of battle and (5) be selective when taking life. The first three principles present the shared ethos of mainstream East Asian social culture; the fourth is common military sense; and the fifth shows inspiration from Buddhism, encouraging nobles not to kill living beings wantonly or needlessly, such as killing animals for sport. Both Kwisan and Ch'uhang exhibited most of these precepts in a conflict with Paekche in 602, rallying the troops after getting caught in a surprise attack, with Kwisan saving his father's life after he was pulled from his horse by a long hook. Both young men died from battle injuries on the road home and were awarded posthumous titles by the Silla king.

General Kim Yusin was a *hwarang* in the early seventh century and, from age fifteen to eighteen, served as leader of a band called the 'Dragon-Flower Aspirants' (*yonghwa hyangdo*), alluding to members of his band seeking rebirth and participation in Maitreya's three assemblies. Numerous legends surround Kim Yusin's desire to protect Silla from its enemies. In one tale he encounters the goddesses of Silla's three sacred mountains, who inform him that among his followers is a Koguryŏ spy. In another tale he receives from a transcendent being a powerful jewelled sword that cuts stone with ease. In a third story, he is taught a 'secret technique' by a supernatural being on Central Peak (Mount Palgong near present-day Taegu) that reportedly enables him to protect Silla from invasions from Koguryŏ and Paekche.

In the decisive battle at Mount Hwangsan in 660, Silla general Hŭmsun sent his son Pan'gul to inspire Silla's forces by offering his life. He said, 'For a vassal, there is nothing greater than fealty; and for a son, there is nothing greater than filial piety. In offering one's life in the face of a crisis, both fealty and filial piety will be realized.' Responding, 'I humbly understand your command,' Pan'gul entered the fierce battle and fought valiantly to the death. After this, Silla's general of the left, P'umil, beckoned his son Kwanch'ang, stood before him in front of his horse, pointed to the arrayed officers and said, 'Although my son is sixteen years old, he has resolve and is courageous. He will be a great model for [our] three armies in today's battle.' Brandishing a spear, Kwanch'ang plunged his armoured horse into the enemy camp. Captured by the defenders, he was taken before Paekche general Kyebaek, who could not bear to kill him after seeing his youth and courage. Kyebaek reportedly sighed and said, 'We are no match for Silla. If their youth are like

Detail of Silla boat-shaped earthenware, Tomb of the Golden Bell, Kyŏngju, 6th century CE.

this, how much more so their mature men?' After returning alive, Kwanch'ang reported to his father, 'When I dashed into the enemy camp, it was not because I feared death that I was unable to kill their general and steal their standard.' Once he finished speaking, he drank some water and headed straight back to the enemy camp. Having captured him once again, Kyebaek beheaded him and sent the youth's head back to his father tied to his horse's saddle.

The *hwarang* order emerged at a crucial time in Silla's history. As it evolved, it functioned to resolve cultural and social pressures between the hereditary elites of Silla and Kaya as the nobles from Kaya were assimilated into Silla's social order. The youth of Silla's expanding state learned their place in the bone-rank system and developed skills and gained experience through the martial and ceremonial activities of the *hwarang*. After Silla's conquests of Koguryŏ and Paekche, through their alliance with Tang China, the military role of the *hwarang* gradually receded and was replaced by increased cultural responsibilities.

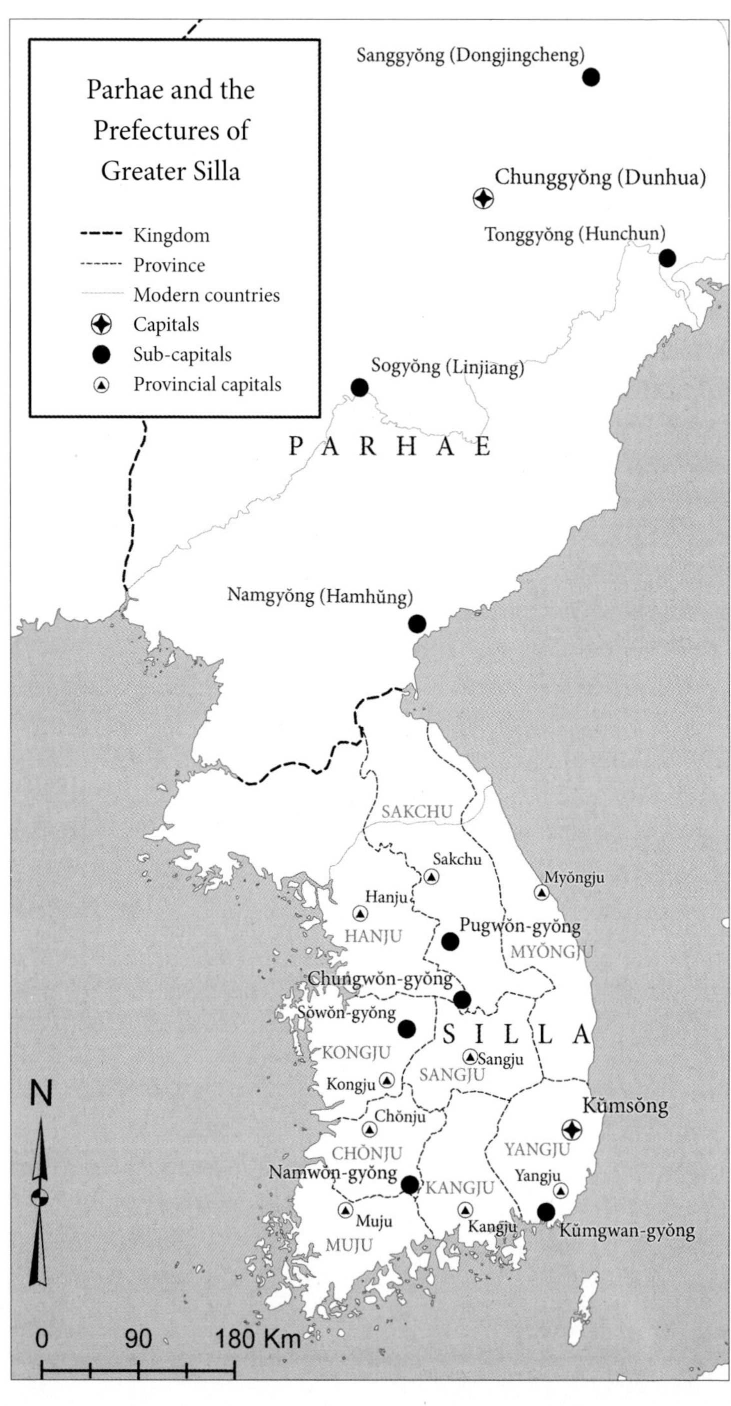
Parhae and the Prefectures of Greater Silla
Kingdom
Province
Modern countries
Capitals
Sub-capitals
Provincial capitals
Sanggyŏng (Dongjingcheng)
Chunggyŏng (Dunhua)
Tonggyŏng (Hunchun)
Sogyŏng (Linjiang)
P A R H A E
Namgyŏng (Hamhŭng)
SAKCHU
Sakchu
Myŏngju
Hanju
HANJU
Pugwŏn-gyŏng
MYŎNGJU
Chungwŏn-gyŏng
Sŏwŏn-gyŏng
S I L L A
KONGJU
Sangju
SANGJU
Kongju
Kŭmsŏng
Chŏnju
YANGJU
CHŎNJU
Namwŏn-gyŏng
KANGJU
Yangju
Muju
Kangju
Kŭmgwan-gyŏng
MUJU
N
0
90
180 Km

FIVE

GREATER SILLA AND PARHAE

The Silla–Tang alliance that brought about the destruction of Paekche and Koguryŏ in the 660s changed the culture and dynamics of the interstate relationships that had existed in Northeast Asia for a few hundred years, perhaps as much as the unification of China under the Sui dynasty in 589 had done in the late sixth century. It ushered in a new period of jockeying for control of territorial domains and the creation of bureaucratic states. For much of the twentieth century, the period from 668 until the demise of Silla in 935 was conventionally called the 'Unified Silla period', following an idea advanced in an influential primer of Korean history composed by a Japanese scholar in the late nineteenth century. In the second half of the twentieth century, however, Korean scholars began to rethink the historical emphasis on Silla, as scholarship on the Koguryŏ connections and influences of the northern state of Parhae (Bohai in Chinese, 698–926) continued to mount. Many Korean scholars now describe the late seventh to tenth centuries as Korea's Northern and Southern Dynasties period, just prior to the rise of the Later Three Kingdoms. Some continue to use 'Unified Silla', but others refer to a 'Greater Silla' to differentiate the Silla state that emerged after the conquests of Paekche and Koguryŏ. In addition, scholars focusing on Silla have returned to the Koryŏ historian Kim Pusik's (1075–1151) periodization of Silla history, which breaks it into early (origins to 654), middle (654–780) and late (780–935) periods, because these blocks of time are better suited to articulating the rise and decline of Silla. Although Silla benefited the most from its association with Tang, having used the

Chinese forces to destroy the defences and capture the capitals of Paekche and Koguryŏ, it was also placed in a precarious situation. The sheer numbers of Tang troops and military leaders on the peninsula may have caused Tang's leaders to rethink prior agreements made with Silla and move to incorporate all of the conquered territories into the Tang administrative system. Chinese historical sources of the period do not describe the original conditions of the Silla–Tang alliance. Korean materials, specifically the Silla annals in the *History of the Three Kingdoms*, preserve a portion of an imperial decree reportedly given to the diplomat Kim Ch'unch'u in 648, which his son, King Munmu (Kim Pŏmmin), quotes in a letter written in 671 responding to accusations of treacherous behaviour advanced by the Chinese general Xue Rengui (614–683):

> Our present attacks on Ko[gu]ryŏ are for but one reason: we take pity on you, Silla, hemmed in by two states, always invaded and humiliated with never a year of peace. Hills, rivers and land I do not covet. Jade and silk [riches] and sons and daughters [people] are things I possess. When we subdue the two states, both [the territory] southward from P'yŏngyang and the land of Paekche will be given to you, Silla, for eternal tranquility.[8]

This passage suggests that Silla understood that Tang emperor Taizong (r. 627–49) originally promised Silla that it would be given all the land of Paekche, and the land of Koguryŏ roughly south of the present-day Taedong river.

The Silla–Tang War and the Consolidation of Silla's Sway over the Peninsula

After Silla and Tang conquered P'yŏngyang, Koguryŏ's capital, their military forces continued to work together to subjugate Koguryŏ military fortresses and strongholds northward in Manchuria. In the seventh lunar month of 671, Tang put down a movement to restore Koguryŏ and, in a letter, the Tang general Xue Rengui accused Silla king Munmu of treachery and complicity by harbouring Koguryŏ fugitives such as Ansŭng, a Koguryŏ noble whom Silla made the lord of Koguryŏ refugees at Hansŏng Fortress in present-day Seoul. Although, according to the *History of the Three Kingdoms*, King Munmu composed a long memorial attempting to mollify the Chinese, asserting that Silla was loyal to Tang rule and reminding Chinese leaders of the agreement between the two countries, and attempted to send it to the imperial court, the message never made it across the Yellow Sea due to rough weather. Paekche fabricated the story that Silla had rebelled against Chinese suzerainty, which arrived in the Tang capital first, so Silla and Tang forces engaged each other as enemies before the end of the year. A factor contributing to the remnant Paekche people's dislike for Silla control was that Silla established Soburi prefecture in Puyŏ, the old Paekche capital, in 671. In 672 Silla moved to consolidate its control over the former Paekche territories, and at the same time dispatched emissaries bearing a memorial and tribute to the Tang court begging for forgiveness and blaming the misunderstanding between the two countries on their bitter enemies in Paekche's lands. Meanwhile, Tang continued to conquer Koguryŏ fortresses that had not yet surrendered. Tang emperor Gaozong (r. 649–83) stripped King Munmu of his title in

Mural featuring a Silla envoy in feathered cap, Tomb of Tang Prince Zhanghuai (Li Xian, 655–84), Qianling, Xi'an, China, late 7th century CE.

674 and attempted to replace him with his brother Kim Inmun (629–694), Silla's resident hostage and political mover and shaker in the Tang capital; he also dispatched several generals and their armies to subdue Silla. Silla installed Prince Ansŭng as King Podŏk of Koguryŏ and prepared to engage the Tang forces with support from remnant armies of Koguryŏ.

A great battle took place between Tang and Silla forces at Maeso Fortress, in present-day Yangju in Kyŏnggi province, in 675. The *History of the Three Kingdoms* claims that Silla was victorious, seizing more than 30,000 warhorses and scores of weapons, but the *Old History of the Tang* reports otherwise, alleging that Tang subdued the Silla rebels. The Korean record also reports that several fortresses in old Koguryŏ territory in present-day Kangwŏn province were besieged by Khitan and Malgal forces serving the Tang. The fortresses held but with considerable losses. The Silla annals also assert that Silla's armies engaged Tang forces in battle eighteen times in 675 and were victorious in all of them. In 676 Silla forces drove the Tang out of the Han river basin, and eventually the Tang withdrew its armies from the Korean peninsula by sea in a fighting retreat at Kibŏlp'o in the eleventh month of that year. Chinese records are curiously quiet about the details of the Silla–Tang conflict and instead focus on a development on Tang's western frontiers that must have been a contributing factor in Silla's seemingly miraculous victories over the Tang imperial forces: Tang's struggles with the emerging Tibetan empire, which had taken control of Tang's military garrisons in the Anxi region, the Tarim basin, in 670 and held them until 692.

The Kim Ch'unch'u Dynasty: Royal Authority and the Strengthening of Autocratic Power

When Kim Ch'unch'u ascended the Silla throne in 654, he adapted Sinitic statecraft practices and Confucian learning to bolster the authority and legitimacy of the Silla king vis-à-vis the powerful hereditary nobility. This was particularly important because both the king and the nobility possessed true-bone (*chin'gol*) status in Silla's bone-rank system, which had become codified during the sixth century. Because Kim Ch'unch'u's direct lineal descendants would rule over Silla until King Hyegong (r. 765–80) suffered regicide in the late eighth century, it is useful to think of the rulers in this period as comprising the Kim Ch'unch'u dynasty. Strengthening the power of the royal family was central to their survival. Although several key bureaucratic organs were instituted during the reigns of King Chinp'yŏng, Queen Sŏndŏk and Queen Chindŏk, such as the Chancellery, Silla rulers did not really replace the seminal function of the council of nobles (*hwabaek*) in guiding and directing the policies of the Silla state until the time of King Muyŏl (Kim Ch'unch'u) and his son King Munmu in the second half of the seventh century. Hitherto, state policies were decided under the direction of the leader of the council, the senior grandee (*sangdaedŭng*), who was conventionally a supporter of the Silla king. The council's decisions, nevertheless, had to be made unanimously. With the growth of the Silla state in the sixth century, the size of the council of nobles swelled to perhaps fifty or more individuals, making unanimous decisions increasingly difficult. Sometime during the reigns of kings Muyŏl and Munmu, however, Silla kings instituted an Administration Chamber, following the political practice established by Tang emperor Gaozu (r. 618–26). Silla's Administration Chamber was probably patterned after its early Tang model: comprising ten to twelve men, headed by three grand councillors and attended by the heads of boards, ministries and other key leaders, such as the director of the Chancellery. Members of the Administration Chamber included prominent nobles and close relatives of the Silla king.

King Munmu's son and successor, King Sinmun, arguably accomplished more in his attempt to curb the power of the hereditary nobles than any other Silla monarch in the Kim Ch'unch'u dynasty. He did this by freely applying Confucian principles and symbolic practices articulated in the 'Royal Regulations' chapter of the *Book of Rites* (*Li ji*). The importance of the 'Royal Regulations' chapter is manifested in his organization of Silla into nine prefectures with a supporting system of five sacred mountains, the institution of an ancestral-temple system focused on five ancestors, and the implementation of an education system centred on learning the Confucian classics and skills of composing literary Sinitic texts in various genres. After suppressing a rebellion instigated by his wife's father, Kim Hŭmdol, in 681, as soon as he ascended the throne, King Sinmun realized that finding and fostering loyal officials would increase royal power and authority, and that this could only be done at the expense of hereditary elites. He implemented several policies to strengthen royal authority.

In 682 he successfully founded a State Academy to deliver a curriculum based on the Confucian classics, which will be treated in greater detail in the following chapter. Although he failed to move the Silla capital to Talgubŏl, present-day Taegu, which was located near the Central Peak (Mount Palgong) in the new structure of five sacred mountains, he was somewhat successful in abolishing the system of stipend villages and establishing an office-land system to allot land to Silla's civil and military officials according to rank, as well as a programme of grain grants, in 688 and 689. These actions were attempts to advance the idea found in Chinese Confucian writings that all land was the king's and that it was his to award to officials, thus promoting royal authority and autocracy.

Silla kings' attempts to curb the power of the hereditary nobility by exerting firmer control over land was a daunting task because the highest-ranking members of the Silla nobility received

Moat in the remains of the Wŏlsŏng Palace Site, Kyŏngju.

Traditional Tomb of General Kim Yusin, Kyŏngju, mid-8th century CE.

'emolument villages', which functioned somewhat like prebendal fiefs, and their families held them in perpetuity. General Kim Yusin, for instance, received five hundred plots of farmland and six horse farms for his services to the state. Of the 174 equestrian facilities and stables existing in Silla in 669, 22 were assigned to the royal family, 10 to government officers, 6 to Kim Yusin (the then reigning king's maternal uncle), 6 to Kim Inmun (the king's younger brother) and the remaining facilities to other high-ranking nobles. The *New History of the Tang* (*Xin Tang shu*) describes, albeit somewhat fantastically, the economic wealth possessed by the highest-ranking officials:

> The house of the Grand Councillor [enjoys] never-ending official pay: 3,000 slaves, armoured troops, oxen, horses and pigs are suitable for one [of his station]. Livestock are pastured on a mountain in the middle of the sea, and when they

> are needed for food, they shoot them with arrows. They loan grain and rice on interest to people, and if they do not repay them in full, it is commonplace for [those people] to become slaves.[9]

King Sinmun's policies on land were formative steps intended to limit the Silla nobility from exercising direct control over the peasant population and to advance the idea of the royal possession of land. Although laconic passages in the *History of the Three Kingdoms* note that land was distributed to adult males in 722 and that an inspector position was established in 748 to assess offences committed by officials, Silla kings' attempts to redefine the land system were doomed to failure because it proved impossible to break the tradition of hereditary privileges enjoyed by the nobility and also because Silla's peasants were economically undeveloped. In 757 King Kyŏngdŏk (r. 742–65) revived the stipend village system and discontinued the office-land and grain grants as the way to pay official salaries, which provides evidence that the royal family was ultimately unable to maintain control over land. Previously, scholars conventionally understood King Kyŏngdŏk's renaming of Silla's office titles in 759 to conform with Tang Chinese patterns as evidence of autocratic rule – and that it pushed 'sinicization' too far – but in reality the promotion of Chinese official titles was superficial because Japan and Parhae also renamed the various titles of their bureaucratic systems following Chinese designations in 758 and 759 respectively. That the power of the hereditary elites had returned previously was acknowledged in 757, and Kyŏngdŏk's son and successor King Hyegong changed the office titles back to their earlier native names in 776.

The Bone-Rank System and Governance in Silla

The hereditary privileges and social limitations of Silla society cannot be understood outside the context of the bone-rank system. This system evolved in the sixth century as a means of ordering Silla society, which was going through profound changes as a result of conquest and the resulting assimilation of tribal peoples, minor polities and communities. All of the early Korean states were socially stratified and based on birth status, but Silla eventually developed systems of social status and ranking more comprehensive than either Koguryŏ or Paekche. The bone-rank system consisted of two bone ranks and six head ranks. At the top was the holy-bone (*sŏnggol*) royal Kim family, but these died out in the mid-seventh century probably due to excessive intermarriage. Other members of the royal Kim family, and powerful capital-based aristocrats surnamed Kim and Pak, generally comprised the second group of true-bone nobles (*chin'gol*). The highest positions in Silla's government were monopolized by true-bone nobles, particularly individuals related to the royal family. The next group were head-rank six elites (*yuktup'um*), comprising capital-based and/or regional elites, often with the surnames Sŏl, Ch'oe, Yi and Chŏng. Although birth barred head-rank six elites from the top positions in Silla's bureaucracy, they compensated by developing their cultural resources – many thus becoming respected and learned Buddhist exegetes and Confucian scholar-officials. The status of the remaining head ranks is speculative because no individuals with these ranks are mentioned in extant literary materials: individuals of head rank five were possibly lower-level regional elites; people of head rank four were possibly local elites; and head ranks three, two and one were likely commoners and slaves. The pre-eminence of the Kim and Pak families is recognized in the following instructive passage from the 'Account of Silla' in the *Old History of the Tang*:

> Their customs, judicial procedures and dress are, for the most part, similar to Ko[gu]ryŏ and Paekche – their court dress remaining plain white. They enjoy offering worship to mountain spirits. For their eating implements they use cups of willow wood. They also use bronze and ceramic [dishes]. Many of the people of the state have the two surnames Kim and Pak, and they are unable to marry anyone with a different surname. They regard the first day [of the year according to the lunar calendar] as important: They congratulate each other and [the king] holds a banquet. Every year on this day they worship

> the spirits of the Sun and the Moon. Furthermore, they also consider the fifteenth day of the eighth month as important: [the king] holds a feast with music and drinking, he rewards his officials, and they display their archery skills in the courtyard. Married women of noble status wear their hair braided in hoops on their head, and for a multicoloured effect they go so far as [using] pearls as hair ornaments. Their hair is extremely long and beautiful.[10]

Although the foregoing passage reports that court dress was primarily white, Korean records report that the true-bone nobles possessing capital ranks 1 to 5 wore purple robes; true-bone nobles and head-rank six elites with capital ranks 6 to 9 wore scarlet robes; nobles and elites, including individuals of head rank five, with capital ranks of 10 to 15 wore blue robes; and nobles and elites with capital ranks 16 and 17 wore yellow robes. This probably reflects the court practices in the eighth and ninth centuries.

Silla nobles were protective of their birth status and differentiated between people of superior, inferior and humble or mean status. Unlike medieval Europe, where children of a nobleman married to a commoner inherited the father's status, in Silla both father and mother needed to possess true-bone status for their children to be considered true-bone. If a true-bone man married or had children with a head-rank six woman, or if a head-rank six man married or had children with a woman possessing true-bone status, any children would inherit head-rank six standing following the parent's lower status. The most famous example is the scholar-official Sŏl Ch'ong (*c.* 660–730), who was the son of the Buddhist monk Wŏnhyo, who possessed head-rank six status, and a widowed true-bone Silla princess. Sŏl Ch'ong inherited his father's head-rank six status.

In the middle of the ninth century, Silla king Hŭngdŏk (r. 826–36) promulgated an edict on clothing, carts and housing that reportedly revived sumptuary regulations that had existed previously in Silla. This pronouncement laid out rules limiting the fabric types, styles and colours of clothing and headgear that could be worn by men and women; the sizes of carts; and the dimensions of homes

Statue of civil official, Kwaenŭng, Tomb of Silla king Wŏnsŏng (r. 785–98), Kyŏngju, late 8th century CE.

that could be possessed by people and families of different bone and head ranks.

Although kings in the line of Kim Ch'unch'u attempted to utilize talented men of head-rank six standing as part of their attempt to break the power of hereditary nobles at court, the succeeding late Silla period (780–935) is characterized by the dominance of the throne by capital-based true-bone nobles and the fraternal competition and strife for power and position in Silla society among such lords possessing hereditary privileges, at the expense of the royal family. In short, Silla monarchs wrestled with their close and distant relatives for control and influence in Silla government and society. During the ninth century, all of the highest positions in government were dominated by true-bone nobles of various Kim lines claiming descent from Silla kings both real and imagined. Although more and more head-rank six elites studied in Tang and returned with real bureaucratic experience, they were increasingly denied access to positions of actual power and authority. This ossification of Silla's ruling elite, limited to true-bone nobles surnamed Kim, was an important factor contributing not only to the dissatisfaction of true-bone nobles deprived of power, but to head-rank six elites eventually turning their support and bureaucratic expertise to regional strongmen when they arose in the late ninth century.

Blame for the decline of Silla is conventionally laid at the feet of Queen Chinsŏng (r. 887–97). Taking at face value the brusque treatment of Chinsŏng in the *History of the Three Kingdoms*, her reputed misbehaviour and poor administration, several scholars have willingly impugned her for the rise of banditry and successful rebellions by Kyŏn Hwŏn (*fl.* 892–936) and Kungye (*fl.* 891–918). It must be remembered, however, that in the roughly 120 years between 768 and 887, the year Chinsŏng ascended the throne, there were at least twenty political upheavals, including significant rebellions by high-ranking Silla nobles such as Kim Hŏnch'ang (822) and his son Kim Pŏmmun (825), as well as the self-made merchant prince Chang Pogo (d. 841 or 846), that attest to the volatile conditions already existing in Silla.

Silla's Interstate Relations with Tang, Japan and Parhae

Silla's relations with Tang were strained throughout the period from the 670s to the early 690s, due to the tension that naturally arose between the two countries after the conquests of Paekche and Koguryŏ. When King Sŏngdŏk (r. 702–37) ascended the

Divine Bell of Silla king Sŏngdŏk (r. 702–37), 771 CE, cast bronze.

throne, he vigorously sought to cultivate a spirit of détente with Tang, dispatching 46 diplomatic and tribute-bearing missions over the course of his long reign. His successors continued the close relations with Tang, so much so that Silla came to be regarded as a civilized, model, tributary state. The *Old History of the Tang* reports that after the passing of King Sŏngdŏk, Tang emperor Xuanzong (r. 712–56) dispatched Xing Shu, a high-ranking official of the Court of State Ceremonial, to Silla to perform rites of mourning for the newly deceased king:

> When [Xing] Shu was about to depart, His Majesty composed an impromptu lyric poem and preface; the heir apparent and all the hundred staff officers in his entourage composed poems and sent them with him. His Majesty instructed Shu, 'Silla may be called a country of gentlemen. They are very knowledgeable about writings and records and are similar to China. Because of your craft in instructing and because you are skilled in lecturing on treatises, you have been selected as the emissary to fulfil this assignment. When you arrive, you should expound and advocate the classics of the Confucian canon and cause them to realize the flourishing of Confucianism in our great country.'[11]

Close and amicable relations with Tang continued until both states fell into decline in the late ninth century.

Chinese culture had been introduced to Japan via the early states on the Korean peninsula, and this continued through the eighth century even after the demise of Paekche, Yamato Japan's ally. Japan's primary interest was the acquisition of Buddhist books and the technologies associated with casting bronze Buddhist images and bells. Silla–Japan relations declined when the Japanese were able to make more direct contact with Tang. Emperor Kanmu (r. 781–806) severed diplomatic relations with Silla in 799; during the ninth century, Japanese pirates frequently raided and plundered the southern coastal regions of Silla, causing a further deterioration of Silla–Japan relations. The Silla native Chang Pogo returned to his homeland from a military career in Tang and, with the king's blessing, in 828 established the Ch'ŏnghae Garrison with 10,000 soldiers on Wan Island off the southwestern coast of Silla. Charged to protect Silla's coasts from pirates as well as to promote Silla's shipping interests, Chang was able to build up a mercantile empire in the mid-ninth century before being assassinated for meddling in the political and dynastic squabbles of the capital-based true-bone nobles by trying to marry his daughter to – and thereby gain powerful influence over – the Silla king.

Silla's relations with the northern kingdom of Parhae were typically strained because they competed with each other for recognition at the Tang court. In 721 the Silla court conscripted 2,000 adult male labourers to build a great long wall at the northern border. When Parhae launched a surprise attack in 733 on the important Tang port city of Dengzhou, on the northern coast of the Shandong peninsula, Tang dispatched Kim Saran, a relative of the Silla king residing in the Chinese capital, to raise troops to repel them. Silla established the P'ae River Garrison in 782 as its northern line of defence against Parhae, and dispatched an emissary to Parhae in 790. Malgal tribal groups subordinate to Parhae sought amicable relations with Silla in the late ninth century.

Silla conducted trading activities with Tang China, primarily, and also with Japan from the mid-seventh century to the mid-ninth. Chinese books, both manuscripts and woodblock prints, were among the most important items acquired in China by both emissarial missions and mercantile ventures. In addition, silk

Dice for drinking game, Wŏlchi, Kyŏngju, 8th century CE.

fabrics, precious metals, ginseng, hunting birds and handicrafts such as paper were among the articles given as gifts or traded in China and Japan. Items traded with Japan usually consisted of plant- and animal-based substances used in dyes and paints, some of which Silla imported from China and other countries in Western Asia. Everyday items and housewares made from brass, and ritual instruments, such as walking sticks with rings, were also among the native products traded with Japan.

The Malgal and the Origins of Parhae

Like Koguryŏ, the way that the state of Parhae (Bohai in Chinese, 698–926) is imagined and conceptualized in scholarship depends on who is telling the story. Chinese scholars tend to claim that Parhae was a feudal regime under Tang dominion. Russian scholars assert that Parhae was an independent kingdom, referred to as the 'flourishing kingdom of the east'. Nevertheless, both Chinese and Russian scholars agree that the rulers of Parhae were Malgal tribespeople. Japanese, North Korean and South Korean scholars, on the other hand, maintain that the ruling elites of Parhae were remnant Koguryŏ military nobles who dominated a commoner class of Malgal peoples. In addition, Korean and Japanese scholars, following the self-identity of Parhae rulers in extant literary sources, generally assert that Parhae was the successor state to Koguryŏ, continuing the multi-ethnic and multicultural traditions established by Koguryŏ in ruling over its vast Manchurian territory. In the second half of the twentieth century, several Korean scholars began referring to the period from the late seventh century to the early tenth as a Korean Northern and Southern Dynasties period, with respect to Silla in the south and Parhae in the north.

The Malgal (Mohe in Chinese) were tribal peoples under the dominion of Koguryŏ prior to its fall. Parhae emerged in the Suifen river basin, the territory of a tribal people called the Uru (Yilou in Chinese), who were ancestors to the Malgal. The ethnic identity of the Malgal is important in the larger view of East Asian history because the Hŭksu Malgal (Heishui Mohe in Chinese) evolved into the Jurchen, who conquered northern China and established the

Convex roof-end tile with a double bird design, Kyŏngju, late 7th–8th century, earthenware.

Jin dynasty (1115–1234). The Jurchen eventually renamed themselves the Manchu and subjugated the whole of China after establishing the Qing dynasty (1644–1912). Thus the ethnic background of Tae Choyŏng, who formed the state in 698, has been a matter of considerable importance to researchers. Tae Choyŏng was most likely an ethnic Malgal fully assimilated to Koguryŏ culture, and thus able to rally support from both the remaining Koguryŏ nobles and Malgal tribespeople. Part of the reason for the confusion about Tae's ethnic status is that Chinese historiographical sources from the tenth and eleventh centuries present conflicting information about the origins of the Parhae state. The *Old History of the Tang* (*Jiu Tang shu*), a pastiche of Tang dynasty materials compiled between 940 and 945, describes the founders of Parhae as a 'branch of Koguryŏ people'. Conversely, the *New History of the Tang*, a completely revised text compiled under the auspices of the literary figure Ouyuang Xiu (1007–1072) between 1043 and 1060, describes the Parhae founder as 'a member of the Malgal that attached himself to Koguryŏ'.

The Growth and Expansion of Parhae

The political history of Parhae can conveniently be broken down into three periods: (1) the founding of the state, (2) expansion period I and (3) expansion period II. The period of state formation spanned much of the reign of Tae Choyŏng (r. 698–719), a former Koguryŏ general, who brought together refugees from Koguryŏ who gathered in present-day Yingzhou. After the fall of Koguryŏ in 668, Tae Choyŏng and his followers eventually had to flee Yingzhou, united with the tribes of the Songmal Malgal (Sumo Mohe) located near the Songhua river, and established a kingdom in the old Koguryŏ domain at Tongmosan (Mount Dongmou), near modern Dunhua in Jilin province. His chief efforts during this early period were to set up defensive measures against the Tang, recover old Koguryŏ lands and bring them under his supervision, and expand his control into the areas of seven Malgal tribes and the Liaodong region. Tae Choyŏng initially named his state Chin-guk; however, early in his reign Tang emperor Xuanzong invested him as 'King of Parhae' in 713.

The first period of expansion spanned the reigns of King Mu (r. 719–37) and King Mun (r. 737–93). King Mu was the first Parhae ruler to declare his own reign title, Inan ('humane peace'). In a diplomatic communication with Japan in 727, recorded in the *Further Chronicles of Japan* (*Shoku Nihongi*), he proudly asserted, 'we have recovered Koguryŏ lands and continued Puyŏ customs.' This is an important piece of evidence suggesting that the Parhae rulers not only viewed themselves as the heirs to Koguryŏ, but, like Koguryŏ and Paekche, sought to legitimize their heritage by laying claim to connections with the earlier Puyŏ state that was destroyed in the mid-fourth century. King Mu moved to subjugate the Hŭksu Malgal located to the north, and also pushed into the southwest, occupying the Liaodong region. He launched an attack on Dengzhou, an important port city and centre of Yellow Sea trade located on the northern side of the Shandong peninsula. This audacious assault in 733 brought an urgent request from Tang for Silla to attack Parhae's southern frontiers, and contributed to the general animosity between Silla and Parhae. Kings Mu and Mun continued to press northward, applying pressure to other Malgal tribes who congregated in the Songhua river region, such as the Chŏlli (Tieli), Puryŏl (Funie), Wŏrhŭi (Yuexi), Uru (Yilou) and Hŭksu (Heishui). In correspondence recorded in Japanese records, King Mun referred to himself as 'king of Koryŏ' – a standard short name for Koguryŏ not to be confused with the later Korean kingdom of Koryŏ (918–1392). In time, however, King Mun envisioned an even grander heritage for himself. In a letter to the Japanese emperor in 771, he asserted that he shared similar exalted status by declaring that he was the 'Grandson of Heaven'.

Parhae's second expansion period occurred during the reign of King Sŏn (r. 818–30), whose reign title, Kŏnhŭng ('rising strong'), echoed the regenerated military power of Parhae. Like his royal forebears, King Sŏn continued to push Parhae's sway northward, subjugating tribes north of Xingkai Lake. Chinese sources attest that 'King Sŏn, Tae Insu, had merit in subjugating the various settlements by the northern sea and expanding his kingdom's territory,'

Warrior and scholar-official Kwaenŭng, Tomb of King Wŏnsŏng (r. 785–98), Kyŏngju, late 8th century CE.

and 'King Sŏn pacified Silla on the south while conquering various settlements in the north, where he established commanderies.'

Both Silla and Parhae selectively adopted and adapted Chinese statecraft and other Sinitic practices, particularly literary culture. Although the evidence is severely limited, most scholars confidently assert that Parhae became even more Sinified than Silla. This was most likely due to an influx of Chinese immigrants looking for land to farm. Parhae king Mun played an important role in crafting the symbolism of royal power and authority. Scholars believe that he established Parhae's system of five capitals, moving the royal and administrative centre of Parhae from the Central Capital to the northern Supreme Capital in 755. The vast expanse of Parhae territory was divided into 15 provinces and 62 districts, with over 100 counties and commanderies. The state dispatched governors (*todok*) and intendents (*chasa*) to supervise its subjects, who were engaged in agriculture as well as hunting and gathering. Commoners called lower-level chiefs *suryŏng* (leader, head).

Parhae Culture

The *Old History of the Tang* reports that Parhae's customs were the same as Koguryŏ's. Korean scholars have taken this to mean that the conventional customs of Parhae society – coming of age, marriage, funerals and memorial rites for ancestors – were the same for the two countries. If the life customs of Parhae were the same as those of Koguryŏ, some scholars intimate that the Parhae language may have been the same as that of Koguryŏ. However, because few examples of Koguryŏ's language remain, and even fewer of Parhae's, this is little more than wishful speculation. Because all the states in Northeast Asia in the seventh, eighth and ninth centuries communicated using a shared written language that is popularly called 'classical or literary Chinese', what historical linguists are increasingly calling 'literary Sinitic', few examples of the vernacular have been preserved. The traditional Korean *ondol* (hypocaust) system for heating underneath the floors of buildings, developed in Koguryŏ, is also found in Parhae royal palaces, suggesting the continuation of Koguryŏ culture in Parhae.

In addition, the Malgal buried their dead in earthen-mound tombs, generally following the practices of Koguryŏ commoners. The Koguryŏ ruling class used stone-lined tombs, stone chambers and stone coffins. Parhae remains show the development of three kinds of tombs: stone, brick and stone chambers covered by earthen mounds. The stone tombs have stone chambers, stone-lined coffins or stone coffins. Brick tombs were made by the royalty from the mid-Parhae period and display influence from Tang China. Tombs with stone chambers covered by an earthen mound, however, were the dominant form in Parhae history, and follow the funerary traditions of Koguryŏ. The funerary culture of Parhae was practical and mortuary practices evolved over the course of the dynasty. It was practical in that numerous sites show evidence of both primary and secondary burials. Primary burial means placing the body of the deceased in the grave or in the ground and sealing it up. Secondary burial means that the body of the deceased is manipulated or changed in some manner before sealing it up in the ground. In some cases, the flesh was removed from bodies first and discarded, and then the bones were buried, but the people of Parhae also practised a form of cremation. The body was placed in a coffin, the coffin was put in the tomb and then the coffin was set on fire. This type of cremation practice, however, disappeared in the mid- to late period. In the early Parhae period, the practice of burying human bones together with animal bones, such as those of horses, cattle and dogs, was widespread. In a few cases, they put buildings up on top of tomb mounds – and later built pagodas – like the General's Tomb in Koguryŏ times.

The official clothing of Parhae's government officials was a mixture of 'inside' or indigenous Korean-style clothing, following old Koguryŏ styles, and 'outside' influences from Tang. Scholar-officials in the nine ranks wore robes of purple, red, light red and green. Officials in the top five ranks carried wooden tablets used to greet royalty (*pu* in Korean, *fu* in Chinese). Tang court robes became increasingly popular from 722. Parhae officials wore purple outer jackets, gold belts and fish pouches, or red outer jackets, silver belts and fish pouches, like the Tang official attire described in the *New History of the Tang*. Everyday clothing appears to have

Funeral urn featuring Tang-style tricolour application technique, Greater Silla, Kyŏngju, 8th century CE.

been loose and comfortable enough to allow those with leisure time to play a football- or soccer-like game (*ch'ukkuk* in Korean, *kemari* in Japanese), and polo, the popular game imported into China and East Asia from the Central Asian steppes. Men wore trousers and a top, hemp headgear, sometimes a conical cap and bird feathers, and leather boots.

The Decline of Parhae

Parhae rule appears to have continued steadily through the reigns of Tae Ijin (r. 830–58) and Tae Kŏnhwang (r. 858–70) in the mid-ninth century. The sources refer to no territorial changes affecting the dynasty. However, internal and external conflict emerged during the rule of Tae Hyŏnsŏk (r. 870–901) and Tae Wihae (r. 901–26). The sources do not elaborate on the nature of the internal difficulties, although some of the same kinds of trouble as were faced by Silla seem likely. In addition, the Hŭksu Malgal revolted against the lords of Parhae. In 886 the Hŭksu Malgal set up a wooden sign expressing the desire to establish peaceful relations with Silla. The Khitans, who had risen to power in northern China in 907, launched a large-scale invasion of Parhae. They surrounded the Parhae capital and, because the royal family had been severely weakened by internal divisions, it surrendered without a fight in the first lunar month of 926. The Parhae king, Tae Insŏn, put on mourning clothes, led sheep out of the gates and surrendered, along with his officials, to the Khitan lord. For the steppe peoples of the north, bringing sheep to a convocation of leaders was a sign of surrender. Prior to the Khitan invasion, in 925, a large number of Parhae subjects, especially high-ranking officials and military leaders, had sought refuge in Koryŏ. The reasons for Parhae's swift collapse are not well known due to the dearth of literary sources. Severe internal conflict among the nobility and governmental elites appears to be a primary cause. Nevertheless, Parhae seems to have maintained its defensive works and strongholds until the Khitan invasion at the end. The quick pace of the Khitan assault strongly suggests that the aggressors knew the locations and understood the strengths and weaknesses of Parhae's defences.

SIX

The Flourishing of Buddhism and Confucianism in Greater Silla

Buddhism and Confucianism became more deeply rooted in Silla society and culture during the middle and late periods (*c.* 654–935), which in this book I refer to as the period of 'Greater Silla'. This chapter charts some of the seminal developments in these traditions. Although surveys of Korean and East Asian history conventionally attempt to make clear distinctions between adherents of Buddhism and of Confucianism, as well as their beliefs, religious practices and social practices, the reality of the relationship between Buddhism, Confucianism, Daoism and other indigenous religious practices was far more complicated in medieval East Asia (*c.* fourth to tenth centuries). For example, the *Book of Trapuṣa* (*Tiwei jing*), a popular apocryphal Buddhist sūtra probably composed in China in about 452, uses mainstream 'Confucian' language to explain the meaning of the five basic precepts that all Buddhists promise to follow: (1) not killing is humaneness, (2) not being adulterous is righteousness, (3) not drinking alcohol is propriety, (4) not stealing is wisdom and (5) proper words spoken (i.e. not lying) is trust. This synthesis of socio-religious mores has been – and in many ways still is – the way Korean people and other East Asians have understood the relationship between religion and society in the context of their shared Sinitic culture.

Standing image of Maitreya, from site of Kamsan Monastery, Kyŏngju, *c.* 720 CE, stone.

Administering the Buddhist Church in Silla

Silla's system for administering the Buddhist church evolved over the course of the dynasty, reflecting the dynamics of the royal family's relationship with the church and officialdom. In the period of mid-antiquity (*c.* 514–654), the religion was governed by literate monastic officials; during the mid-Silla period (654–780), it was administered by secular officials; and during the late Silla period (780–935), it was managed by a hybrid system of monastic and secular officials. In the second half of the sixth century, monastic officials based in the Silla capital bore titles such as state Buddhist overseer (*kukt'ong*) and chief Buddhist nun (*toyunanang*), both of which attest to influence from the Buddhist administrations of the Chinese Northern Dynasties, which was probably mediated through Koguryŏ influence.

The Office of the Great Religion, run by secular officials, was probably first organized by King Chinp'yŏng (r. 579–632) and made subordinate to the Board of Rites in 594. Because the head office of great Buddhist rectifier (*taejŏng*) could be held by someone bearing a capital rank from *kŭpch'an* (rank 9) up to *ach'an* (rank 6), it is thought that such a person was not a world-renouncing monk – not to mention various secular scribes and secretaries. The administrative duties of the Office of the Great Religion included protection and control of the Buddhist church, including management of renunciant monks and nuns and the *saṃgha* register, the founding and renovation of monasteries, the production of Buddhist images and pagodas and the holding of assemblies and ceremonies. When the eminent monk Chajang (*fl.* 636–50) returned from Tang China in 643, he was made the great state Buddhist overseer (*taegukt'ong*), a special office bestowed solely on him, and he instituted more rigorous controls over monastic behaviour by installing touring commissioners to teach appropriate discipline to monks and nuns in prefectural monasteries. Chajang also lectured on the *Flower Garland Sūtra* (*Huayan jing*) and, according to later narratives, recognized Mount Odae (Korea's Mount Wutai) as the local abode of the Bodhisattva Mañjuśrī through several spiritual encounters on the mountain.

The massive state palladium Hwangnyong Monastery had served as the locus of state protection rituals from its founding in 553 to the building of the nine-storey wooden pagoda in 645 under Chajang's direction. After Chajang's passing, and during the mid-Silla period, the relative importance of Hwangnyong Monastery declined and the administrative responsibility for managing Buddhist rituals and votive offerings for the benefit of deceased rulers and their like was transferred to four managerial departments that oversaw monasteries during the late seventh century. Separate managerial departments supervised Sach'ŏnwang Monastery, Pongsŏng Monastery, Kamŭn Monastery and Pongdŏk Monastery in the Silla capital. Hwangnyong Monastery regained importance in the late Silla period as the chief 'state monastic complex' (*kukch'al*).

Members of the royal Kim family of Silla were generous patrons of the Buddhist church, and typically held lavish ceremonies supervised by state preceptors (*kuksa*), although a few kings limited the performance of ceremonies and rituals by subjects that were financially reckless. As royal power declined in the late Silla period, kings attempted to draw upon the charisma of Zen (Sŏn) masters to bolster their declining authority. The hybrid system of utilizing

Site of Hwangnyong Monastery, Kyŏngju.

both monastic and secular officials to govern the Buddhist church pre-dated the crowning achievement: the institution of the Office for the Administration of the Dharma. State authority and the Buddhist church were closely integrated in Silla between the seventh and tenth centuries, based on the total subordination of the Buddhist church to state authority. Despite this, leaders of the Buddhist church in Silla do not seem to have considered the relationship as excessive or oppressive.

Wŏnhyo and Doctrinal Buddhism

Wŏnhyo (617–686) was one of the most prolific and revered monks in medieval East Asia. His secular surname was Sŏl, and he possessed head-rank six status in Silla's bone-rank system. Born in what is present-day Kyŏngsan, in North Kyŏngsang province, he travelled to the capital and resided, for a time, at Punhwang Monastery, located just north of the hub of scholarly Buddhism at Hwangnyong Monastery. Naturally brilliant and insightful, he possessed a comprehensive understanding of the major sūtras, commentaries and treatises translated into or composed in literary Sinitic that existed in his time. Like other monastic exegetes, he participated in the flourishing Buddhist intellectual culture of the time by writing commentaries on all of the major sūtras and treatises. He is believed to have composed 99 titles in 240 rolls, though only 22 works have been preserved. Numerous Buddhist sūtras had been translated into literary Sinitic, and scholar monks sought to organize the various and sometimes contradictory doctrines and practices advanced in these sūtras and treatises into understandable and practicable schemes. In this context, he was familiar with the writings of Tiantai Zhiyi (538–597), founder of the Chinese Tiantai school, who privileged the role of the *Lotus Sūtra* in his scheme. Wŏnhyo influenced Chinese Huayan master Fazang (643–712), and one of Wŏnhyo's two extant commentaries on the *Treatise on Awakening Mahāyāna Faith* (*Dasheng qixin lun*) is famously known throughout East Asia as the *Korean Commentary* (*Haedong so*).

Wŏnhyo's initial training must have included Madhyamaka, which emphasized the doctrine of emptiness (the lack of self or anything that pertains to a self in the six senses and their objects) and that no doctrinal position could be established, and Yogācāra, which in contradistinction to Madhyamaka posited the functioning of the mind, 'mind-only' or 'consciousness-only', and that emptiness must be understood in terms of three aspects of mind. In sixth- and seventh-century China, proponents of Yogācāra were divided into the Dilun school, which followed the *Treatise on the Sūtra concerning the Ten Stages* (*Dilun*), and the Shelun school, based on the *Treatise on Embracing the Mahāyāna* (*Shelun*). The Dilun school evolved into the Huayan school and held that all beings could progress on the path of the ten bodhisattva stages towards Buddhahood. The more conservative Shelun school held that some living beings, called *icchantika*, were incapable of becoming awakened because the deep level of their 'storehouse consciousness' was polluted with bad seeds. Although Wŏnhyo was intimately familiar with both commentaries, and was a Shelun proponent of a kind, he also believed that all beings possess Buddha-nature and its concomitant potential for Buddhahood. One of the Indian doctrines rising in importance in the seventh century was that of the *Tathāgatagarbha*, 'the embryo or womb of Buddhahood', which posited that all living beings have a pure embryo or womb within them that ultimately enables them to attain Buddhahood. This combined with the similar East Asian doctrine that all beings possess Buddha-nature or have the innate potential for Buddhahood. Wŏnhyo was a proponent of these teachings, which became the dominant doctrinal position held in East Asia thereafter. He fleshed out his views in commentaries on such works as the *Awakening of Faith*, the *Flower Garland Sūtra*, the *Lotus Sūtra* and the apocryphal *Vajrasamādhi Sūtra*. Some of his scholarly writings, the *Treatise on the Vajrasamadhi Sūtra* (*Kŭmgang sammae-gyŏng non*) and *Treatise on the Reconciliation of Disputes in Ten Approaches* (*Simmun hwajaeng non*), were so well received by other Buddhist scholiasts that they were raised to the status of 'treatise', like the writings of the great Indian Buddhist masters.

A badly damaged early ninth-century stele with a partially readable inscription commemorating Wŏnhyo's achievements was found at the site of Kosŏn Monastery, east of Kyŏngju. The inscription refers to Wŏnhyo's *Doctrinal Essentials of the Flower Garland*

Ridge-end ornament, from site of Hwangnyong Monastery, Kyŏngju, 7th century CE.

Sūtra (*Hwaŏm chongyo*) as one of his chief writings. Although this has been completely lost, the preface and roll three of his *Commentary on the Flower Garland Sūtra* (*Hwaŏm so*) have been preserved. Hagiographers emphasized Wŏnhyo's alternative approaches to making Buddhist truths accessible to the people of Silla: he played the zither, sang songs and danced wearing a large gourd mask called 'Unhindered' (*muae*) after a teaching in the *Flower Garland Sūtra*. He wrote and preached about venerating Maitreya, the future Buddha, and Amitābha, the Buddha of Western Paradise, all the while encouraging ordinary people to arouse their aspiration to enlightenment and become bodhisattva adherents of the Mahāyāna. Wŏnhyo's fame and writings spread to Japan, where he, along with his friend Ŭisang, was considered a founder of the East Asian Huayan school (Hwaŏm in Korean, Kegon in Japanese) based on the *Flower Garland Sūtra*.

Ŭisang and the Birth of the Hwaŏm Tradition

Wŏnhyo's younger friend and colleague Ŭisang (625–702) travelled to Tang and ultimately studied with the early Huayan master Zhiyan (602–668) along with the previously mentioned Fazang. For the remainder of their lives, Ŭisang and Fazang kept in touch via letters carried by Silla students going back and forth to study Buddhism in Tang. While Fazang went on to become one of the most important doctrinal thinkers of the Chinese Buddhist tradition, Ŭisang distinguished himself primarily as a practitioner and trainer of students. Although earlier eminent monks, such as Chajang, previously lectured on the *Flower Garland Sūtra*, Ŭisang was remembered in Silla as the founder of the dominant Hwaŏm school.

Nevertheless, one of Ŭisang's extant writings, the *Seal-Diagram Symbolizing the Dharma Realm of the One Vehicle* (*Hwaŏm ilsŭng pŏpkye to*) and its auto-commentary, is a brilliant example of the Buddhist scholarly creativity of seventh-century East Asia. The *Seal-Diagram* comprises a *gāthā* (religious song or poem) in 210 sinographs, 30 lines of heptasyllabic verse, written in literary Sinitic and organized into a meandering seal shape so that the beginning and the end meet in the centre of the diagram. The *gāthā* summarizes the core teachings of the sixty-roll edition of the *Flower Garland Sūtra*: the principles of interfusion and integration, the 'one containing the many' and the 'many containing the one', and the 'ocean-seal meditative absorption' (*haein sammae*), and it inspires practitioners to arouse their aspiration to enlightenment and acquire *dhāraṇīs* (Sanskrit spells and incantations) that endow bodhisattvas with the ability to work wonders that benefit themselves and others on the path towards Buddhahood in the mundane world. Scholarly commentary on Ŭisang's *Seal-Diagram* was a key intellectual pursuit for several centuries in Korea, and the importance of this meaningful diagram continues to the present day.

Ŭisang lectured on the *Flower Garland Sūtra* immediately after returning to Silla in 671. Leading his disciples to a place called Awl Grotto (Ch'udong) on Mount Sobaek, he lectured on the *Flower Garland Sūtra* for several days to benefit the recently deceased mother of one of his main followers. He founded Pusŏk Monastery on Mount T'aebaek by royal command in 676 and recognized the importance of other sacred sites on the peninsula. Ŭisang's practice combined veneration of the *Flower Garland Sūtra* with the popular cults of the Buddha Amitābha and the Bodhisattva Avalokiteśvara. Ŭisang's ten great disciples went on to found Buddhist monastic complexes throughout Silla, and Hwaŏm-oriented monasteries were built on each of the five sacred mountains of Silla: Pulguk Monastery on the Eastern Peak (Mount T'oham), Su Monastery on the Western Peak (Mount Kyeryong), Hwaŏm Monastery on the Southern Peak (Mount Chiri), Pusŏk Monastery on the Northern Peak (Mount T'aebaek) and Miri Monastery on the Central Peak (Mount Palgong).

The Silla royal family utilized rituals associated with the Hwaŏm cult on Mount Odae (Five Terrace Mountain) to bolster their symbolic authority and supplicate the buddhas for protection and

Śarīra reliquary, east pagoda of Kamŭn Monastery Site, Greater Silla, *c.* 682 CE, gilt bronze.

success beginning in the eighth century. According to tradition, Poch'ŏn (*fl.* 692–737), a son of King Sinmun, founded True Suchness Cloister on the central peak or terrace of Mount Odae, and the royal family went on to erect shrines to the great bodhisattvas and buddhas mentioned in the *Flower Garland Sūtra* on the remaining terraces. Special rituals, including the Flower Garland Convocation, were held by monastic acolytes yearly in these shrines during the eighth and ninth centuries. Veneration of the gods comprising the Divine Assembly, the deities, bodhisattvas and supernatural beings who listened to the preaching of the *Flower Garland Sūtra* also flourished in eighth- to tenth-century Silla, particularly at Haeinsa (Ocean Seal Monastery) on Mount Kaya, which was built in the early ninth century and named for the 'ocean-seal meditative absorption'. Anecdotes regarding monks and lay believers who practised the 'flower garland meditative absorption' (*hwaŏm sammae*) illustrate how the gods of the Divine Assembly were invoked to protect not only monastic complexes but the entire land of Silla. Hwaŏm societies for the veneration of Ŭisang and other important founders of the East Asian Hwaŏm tradition were also active in the late Silla period. Vow texts composed by the scholar Ch'oe Ch'iwŏn for such commemoration rituals have been preserved from the late ninth century, showing the importance of the Hwaŏm tradition in the ninth and tenth centuries.

The Cult of Amitābha and Devotional Narratives

During the late sixth century and the seventh, worship of Amitābha, the Buddha of the Western Paradise Sukhāvatī, began to replace adoration of the future Buddha Maitreya as the most popular Buddhist cult in East Asia. The sūtras associated with Amitābha's Pure Land describe it as a place perfect for making spiritual progress. However, the quality of rebirth in the Pure Land differs according to the spiritual capacities and attainments of aspirants. There are three levels or grades of rebirth – superior, middling and inferior – and each of these three is further subdivided into a superior, middling and inferior class. The core practices of the nascent Amitābha cult in Silla, like those in medieval China, were 'recollection of the

Buddha [Amitābha]' (*yŏmbul, nianfo* in Chinese) and '[recollection of Amitābha for] ten thought-moments' (*simnyŏn*), which caused rebirth in the Pure Land. Scholar monks understood these ideally as powerful meditative practices for advanced practitioners to be performed concomitantly with arousing the aspiration to enlightenment and becoming a bodhisattva. Such behaviour enables someone to be born in the superior class. Ordinary people with limited spiritual capacity were encouraged to simply chant the name of Amitābha for ten thought-moments or ten times to be reborn in the lowest grade of the lowest class in Amitābha's Pure Land. The Chinese monk Shandao (613–681) glossed 'ten thought-moments' as 'ten intonations' (*shisheng, sipsŏng* in Korean), and his interpretation of the practice simplified to vocal recitation became increasingly accepted by scholar monks in East Asia (including Silla) to the extent that 'recollection of the Buddha Amitābha' has since become synonymous with 'chanting the name of the Buddha Amitābha'.

Seated buddha and attendant bodhisattva, Buddha Rock (*Puchŏ pawi*), Namsan, Kyŏngju, 7th century CE.

Iryŏn's *Memorabilia of the Three Kingdoms* preserves numerous stories of monks and lay believers seeking rebirth in Amitābha's Pure Land. The story of the friends Kwangdŏk and Ŏmjang illustrates the earlier, more meditative, approach to Pure Land practice. Kwangdŏk and his wife practised verbal recitation of Amitābha's name as well as the sixteen visualizations of the *Sūtra on the Visualization of the Buddha Amitāyus* (*Guan Wuliangshou jing*). After Kwangdŏk passed away, his friend Ŏmjang offered to take his friend's wife into his home. Later that evening, Ŏmjang made sexual advances towards Kwangdŏk's wife, and she reproved him, informing him of her late husband's abstinence and their steadfast practice of the visualizations following the moon's journey to the western region. She encouraged Ŏmjang to seek out Wŏnhyo for training. Ŏmjang followed her advice and attained rebirth in the Pure Land when he died. This narrative preserves a native song (*hyangga*) in the Silla vernacular attributed to Kwangdŏk:

> O Moon, now,
> Go to the West,
> And in front of Amitābha,
> Please tell that there is one who adores him,
> Buddha of Limitless Life and Vow,
> And prays before him with folded hands,
> That he may be reborn immediately into his Pure Land.
> If this flesh is not left behind,
> Can your forty-eight vows be met?[12]

By the middle of the eighth century, verbal recitation of Amitābha's name had spread throughout all social strata, and the people of Silla developed indigenous ways of worshipping this great Buddha. One such narrative centres on the slave woman Ungmyŏn who lived during the reign of King Kyŏngdŏk (742–65). She would follow her master to Mit'asa (Amitābha Monastery) in what is present-day Chinju in South Kyŏngsang province. There scores of believers would make 'binding oaths for ten thousand days'. Although her master forbade her from going, and gave her extra chores to keep her busy, such was her diligence and faith that she

Pulguk Monastery, Mt T'oham, Kyŏngju.

went to the monastery after finishing her chores and recited Amitābha's name fervently. As a display of devotion, she bored holes through the palms of her hands and affixed a rope through them connected to opposite ends of the monastery's courtyard. One evening, heavenly chanting was heard inviting her to 'ascend into the hall and recite the name of Buddha'. Heavenly music filled the air, and she was whirled away to the West, transformed into a perfected form. Although most laypeople who venerated Amitābha did not perform such ascetic practices, Ten-Thousand-Day Assemblies for invoking and chanting the name of Amitābha appear to have spread throughout Silla in the eighth and ninth centuries.

Buddhist devotional literature, like that of Confucian-oriented narratives that will be treated briefly below, comprised stories that illustrated the integration of Buddhist doctrines, beliefs and practices and mainstream social mores into ordinary people's everyday lives. Here I will paraphrase the account of the Silla noble Kim

Taesŏng (d. 775), who is remembered for commissioning the famous Pulguk Monastery and Sŏkkuram Grotto, two of the crowning achievements of Silla Buddhist architecture. According to *Memorabilia of the Three Kingdoms*, during the reign of King Sinmun there was a poor woman named Kyŏngjo, whose son had a large and flat forehead, so he was called Taesŏng (Great Wall). Because his family was poor, he laboured in the fields for a local rich man. One day a Buddhist monk came by begging for money to hold a special dharma assembly. The rich man made a generous donation and Taesŏng overhead the monk promise, by means of an incantation, that the rich man would be rewarded ten-thousand-fold. Taesŏng returned home excitedly and told his mother that their family had such continual economic suffering because it had not made donations to the Buddhist church.

Consumed by his desire to make a generous offering, Taesŏng died not long thereafter. On the night of his death, a voice emanating from heaven was heard at the mansion of Kim Mullyang, director of the Chancellery. It announced that Taesŏng of Moryang Village would be reborn into Director Kim's family. Servants were sent to clarify the details and verify the death of Taesŏng, and in due time, Director Kim's wife conceived and gave birth to a son. The baby held his left hand clenched tightly for seven days, and when he finally opened it, he was holding a golden tablet with the sinographs 'Taesŏng' carved on it. For this reason, Director Kim named the boy Taesŏng and brought his mother from his previous lifetime into their home and took care of her. Taesŏng liked to hunt while he was growing up, but after catching a bear near sacred Mount T'oham, he dreamed that the bear changed into a ghost and threatened to eat him in a future lifetime. Taesŏng asked the bear's forgiveness and promised to construct a monastery on the bear's behalf, Changsu Monastery, on the site where he had killed the bear. Displaying Buddhist-inspired filial piety and the desire to earn merit for his parents from two lifetimes, he then built Pulguk Monastery for his parents in his present life (Kim Mullyang and his wife), and Sŏkpul Monastery (now called Sŏkkuram) for his parents in his previous life (Kyŏngjo). Construction on Pulguk Monastery began in 751, and neither had been fully completed when Kim Taesŏng died on the

Sŏkkuram, frontal view of main chamber, Mt T'oham, Kyŏngju, *c.* 775 CE.

second day of the twelfth month of the *kabin* year (8 January 775). The Silla government then took over and completed the monastery, the architecture of which integrates the worship of Amitābha with the veneration of Vairocana, the chief Buddha of the *Flower Garland Sūtra*, who symbolizes the universe itself. Sŏkkuram Grotto, which also presents a Hwaŏm-inspired snapshot of the universe, looks as though the court decided to leave it slightly unfinished since some of the carved stone images in the grotto are roughly hewn and less detailed than others.

The Mountain Schools of Sŏn Buddhism

Zen Buddhism (Chan in Chinese, Sŏn in Korean) developed in China during the Tang period as a kind of reform movement and refutation of doctrinal Buddhism. In a simple sense, proponents sought to emphasize meditative practice over scriptural learning. Drawing on expressions utilizing the rich language and heritage of Sinitic culture (including Daoism) – and eschewing Indian- and Sanskrit-inspired doctrinal terms – proponents advanced the rhetoric that their approach to practice was superior to the study of Buddhist sūtras and commentaries because it did not rely on words. Zen masters also claimed that generous patronage of the Buddhist church was ultimately ineffective in seeking liberation from the cycle of rebirth and death, and that one should only engage in meditative practices that will catalyse 'seeing one's true nature' (*kyŏnsŏng*), enabling one to attain Buddhahood immediately. Early Zen masters in eighth-century China also dabbled in non-verbal practices, such as shouts and blows, to shock their students out of their normal ways of thinking. Despite the rhetoric, the idea that people can see their true nature is firmly based on the mainstream doctrine of the *Tathāgatagarbha*, that all beings possess Buddha-nature. In addition, the quality and portrayal of enlightenment espoused by the Zen masters corresponds to the description of ultimate reality articulated in the *Flower Garland Sūtra*. Sŏn (Zen) traditions came into Silla when the Hwaŏm school was dominant at court and in the countryside. The complex and fruitful combination of Hwaŏm and Sŏn has been key to the development of Korea's Buddhist traditions from the eighth century to the present.

Pŏmnang (*fl.* mid-seventh century) was the first Silla monk said to have transmitted the teaching of Chan (Zen) master Daoxin (580–651), and Pŏmnang may even have composed the apocryphal *Vajrasamādhi Sūtra* made famous by Wŏnhyo's treatise. But Daoxin's Zen, later called 'Northern School' and deemed to emphasize an inferior 'gradual' practice as opposed to the superior 'sudden' practice of the Southern School, never really caught on in Silla. Neither did that of Sinhaeng (704–779), who is also said to have brought back the inferior 'gradual' Zen of the Northern School.

According to the conventionally accepted narrative deriving from inscriptions on a funerary stele of eminent Zen monks of Silla, Zen only began to take root in Silla when a series of monks who studied the Zen of the Southern School returned to their homeland. Toŭi (dates unknown) left for Tang in 784, Hyeso (744–850) in 824, Hyech'ŏl (797–868) in 814, Muyŏm (801–888) in 821, Hyŏnuk (787–868) in 824, Toyun (797–868) in 825 and Ch'ejing (804–880)

Seated Vairocana, Top'ian Monastery, Ch'ŏrwŏn, Kangwŏn Province, 865 CE.

in 837. They returned to Silla, beginning with Toŭi in 821, followed by Hyeso in 830, Hyŏnuk in 837, Hyech'ŏl in 839 and Ch'ejing in 840. Other monks returned after the great Huichang persecution of Buddhism in Tang, when many of the great monastic complexes of the Tang capital, Chang'an, were dismantled: Muyŏm in 845, Pŏmil (810–894) in 846 and Toyun in 847.

Toŭi was taught by Xitang Zhizang (735–814), who studied under the famous Zen master Mazu Daoyi (709–788), and was the first monk to spread Southern School Zen in Silla. Originally trained in the Hwaŏm school, he realized that spreading Zen in Silla would be difficult due to the strong hold of the doctrinal traditions and their popular ritual practices. He transmitted his teaching to Yŏmgŏ (d. 844) and sought seclusion in the mountains. Hongch'ŏk (dates unknown) also studied under Xitang, returned to Silla in 826 and acquired the support of the Silla king. He began spreading the Zen teaching at Silsang Monastery on Mount Chiri in present-day Namwŏn in South Chŏlla province. He is remembered as the founder of the Mount Silsang monastery school. The early Korean Zen traditions, conventionally called the 'Sŏn Schools of the Nine Mountains' in the Koryŏ period (918–1392), were founded at monasteries far from the Silla capital in present-day Chŏlla, Ch'ungch'ŏng and Kangwŏn provinces. Although many Silla monks who studied Zen in Tang were favoured by Silla kings, who sought to utilize their charisma to support their waning authority, the founders of these mountain schools were typically supported by local strongmen, who began to rise in the second half of the ninth century. Zen eventually became the dominant Buddhist tradition in Korea in the thirteenth century during the Koryŏ period.

Confucianism in Silla in the Context of Early Korea

Confucianism entered the Korean peninsula gradually as part of the complex and multifaceted package or bundle of Sinitic culture which was transmitted by emissaries, immigrants, Buddhist monks, merchants and student scholars. In medieval China (*c.* 317–907), Confucianism was not parochial or dogmatic, as the mature form may have appeared to Western visitors to East Asia, particularly

China and Korea, in the eighteenth, nineteenth and early twentieth centuries – and it was not a 'religion' focused on the worship of Confucius. The Sinitic term conventionally translated as 'Confucianism', *yugyo* in Korean (*rujiao* in Chinese), literally means 'the teaching of the scholars'. Simply stated, the Confucianism of this time was associated with the procedures and principles for ruling a state and governing a family. Confucius (551–479 BCE) was commemorated with sacrifices as the exemplar educator, who encouraged rulers of states to look to the model leaders of antiquity and to fortify the cultural foundations of education and moral behaviour as the best means for causing the people and the state to flourish.

By the early centuries of the Common Era, Confucianism in East Asia was associated with a body of literature that was held to convey the keys to good government and education. This literature included the *Book of Songs*, the *Book of Documents*, the *Book of Rites*, the *Book of Changes* and the *Spring and Autumn Annals*, which are traditionally considered to have been compiled or edited by Confucius and thus are conventionally regarded as the 'Confucian classics' along with a *Book of Music* that was lost in antiquity. Chinese literature from the Han (*c.* 206 BCE–220 CE) and Three Kingdoms (220–80) periods refers to 'seven classics', but does not mention the precise titles of the works. Sources dating from the Tang period commonly refer to 'nine classics', but the titles of the nine differ according to author. In the ninth century, Tang emperor Wenzong (r. 827–40) commissioned the carving of twelve Confucian texts in stone during the Kaicheng reign period (833–7). This list conforms relatively closely to the list of thirteen classics studied for the state-administered civil service examinations of the succeeding Song period (960–1279): (1) the *Book of Changes* (*Yijing*), (2) the *Book of Documents* (*Shujing*) and (3) the *Book of Songs* (*Shijing*); the three 'ritual' texts (4) the *Rites of Zhou* (*Zhouli*), (5) *Ceremonies and Rites* (*Yili*) and (6) the *Book of Rites* (*Liji*); the three commentaries to the *Spring and Autumn Annals* (7) the *Zuo Commentary* (*Zuozhuan*), (8) the *Gongyang Commentary* (*Gongyang zhuan*) and (9) the *Guliang Commentary* (*Guliang zhuan*); and (10) the *Analects* (*Lunyu*), (11) the *Book of Filial Piety* (*Xiaojing*),

(12) the dictionary *Approaching Elegance* (*Erya*) and (13) the *Mencius* (*Mengzi*).

Study of these texts was closely associated with literacy, and some of these texts served as models for literary composition, although by the medieval period Sinitic literary culture had evolved to the extent that books such as the *Analects*, the *Mencius* and the *Book of Filial Piety*, along with the so-called 'Daoist' *Daode jing* and *Zhuangzi*, were part of the basic curricula with which all generally educated people were familiar to some extent, in much the same way as *Pride and Prejudice*, *Frankenstein*, *The Great Gatsby* and *To Kill a Mockingbird* are staples of literature courses in many schools in the English-speaking world.

Texts such as the *Analects*, a collection of Confucius' teachings on various subjects compiled by his later disciples, and the *Mencius*, the teachings of the second most famous Confucian scholar Mengzi (Meng Ke, *c.* 372–289 BCE), articulate key concepts associated with the Confucian approach to life: humaneness, propriety and ceremony, fealty or righteousness, reciprocity or mutual consideration, loyalty, the rectification of names, the gentleman and so forth. For instance, the *Mencius* codifies the five moral relations: fealty (or rightness or righteousness) should exist between ruler and subject, intimacy (or closeness) between father and son, distinction (or separation of duties) between husband and wife, precedence between older and younger, and confidence (or trust) between friends. These became the backbone of Confucian social and political mores. Texts such as the *Book of Documents* communicated such concepts as the Mandate of Heaven, which functioned as a way of explaining how and justifying why dynasties collapsed through the symbiotic interplay between heaven, earth and man. Ritual texts, such as the *Book of Rites*, formulated rules and procedures for appropriately commemorating ancestors, venerating the gods and spirits of mountains and rivers, and supplicating the gods of soil and grain. It also provided guidelines for rulers on how to organize educational institutions.

Confucian Education and Scholarship and Silla's State Academy

Koguryŏ established a State Academy (*t'aehak*) in 372, and although we do not know the curriculum, it likely consisted of the five core Confucian classics and the two early histories, the *Records of the Grand Historian* (*Shiji*) and the *History of the Former Han* (*Han shu*), as well as the *Selections of Refined Literature* (*Wenxuan*), after it was compiled between 520 and 530 by the Liang prince Xiao Tong (501–531). In addition to the State Academy, the account of Koguryŏ in the *Old History of the Tang* briefly describes the existence of an institution called the *kyŏngdang*, a school for unmarried young men. Likely established as a provincial feeder mechanism for noble youths to be sent on to the State Academy, most were probably established after the Koguryŏ capital was transferred to P'yŏngyang in 427. In locally established *kyŏngdang*, the young men comprising garrisoned military units read books and practised archery. Scholars hypothesize that students cultivated Confucian-inspired moral virtues and martial skills under the supervision of the local fortress authority or castle lord (*sŏngju*). Considering Koguryŏ's political and cultural influence over Silla during the fourth and fifth centuries, some scholars suspect that the *kyŏngdang* institution influenced or became a model for Silla's *hwarang* organization.

Like other states in Northeast Asia, educated elites in Koguryŏ and Paekche were called 'erudites' (*paksa*), the same word used for 'doctors of philosophy' in modern East Asian languages. In 600 the Koguryŏ erudite Yi Munjin re-edited the hundred rolls of *Preserved Records* (*Yugi*), creating a condensed five-roll text called the *New Collection* (*Sinjip*). The Paekche erudite Ko Hŭng, who was probably an immigrant from China, compiled *Documentary Records* (*Sŏgi*) during the reign of King Kŭnch'ogo (346–75). Japanese texts, such as the *Chronicles of Japan*, report that other Paekche erudites, such as Wang In (dates unknown), Tan Yangi (*fl.* 513) and Ko Anmu (*fl.* 516), were specialists in the five Confucian classics and crossed over to Japan to teach the skills of reading and composition in literary Sinitic. The Silla noble Kŏch'ilbu (*fl.* 540–79) compiled the first *State History* (*Kuksa*) of Silla in 545.

Following guidelines for rulers in the 'Royal Regulations' chapter of the *Book of Rites*, Silla king Sinmun established Silla's State Academy (*kukhak*) early in his reign in 682. The Koryŏ scholar-official and historian Kim Pusik described the educational curriculum of the State Academy as follows. The standard course of study was the *Book of Changes*, the *Book of Documents*, Mao's (version of the) *Book of Poetry*, the *Book of Rites*, the *Zuo Commentary of the Spring and Autumn Annals* and *Selections of Refined Literature*. An erudite or instructor could also supplement the study of two or three of these core texts with the *Analects* and the *Book of Filial Piety*. Graduates of Silla's State Academy were grouped into three rankings: high, middle and low. Those who could read the *Zuo Commentary*, the *Book of Rites* or *Selections of Refined Literature*, and were able to comprehend and elucidate on the *Analects* and the *Book of Filial Piety*, were graduated in the high ranking; those who read *Minutiae of Etiquette* (*Qu li*), the *Analects* and the *Book of Filial Piety* were graduated in the middle ranking; and those who read the *Minutiae of Etiquette* and the *Book of Filial Piety* were graduated in the low ranking. Students who demonstrated complete comprehension of the Five Classics, the Three Histories (the *Records of the Grand Historian*, the *History of the Former Han* and the *History of the Later Han*) and the writings of the Hundred Schools of Philosophers (which included the *Analects*, the *Mencius*, *Xunzi*, *Han Feizi* and so on) were immediately selected for employment by the state. Silla's State Academy also had a mathematics course of study where instructors taught four books on mathematical principles and problems.

The rise of Confucianism in early Korea is inextricably tied to the emergence of literary culture in Silla. When Kim Ch'unch'u went to Tang as an emissary in 648, he requested to visit the Imperial University, observe the rituals commemorating Confucius (*shidian*, *sŏkchon* in Korean) and hear lectures on the *Analects*. Recognizing Silla's interest in Tang literary culture, Emperor Taizong (r. 626–49) bestowed upon him copies of the finest examples of literary composition, scholarship and calligraphy of the age: the 'Stele Inscription of the Warm Hot Springs' ('Wen tang'), written by Taizong's father, Emperor Gaozu, when he travelled to the hot springs at

Lishan; the 'Stele Inscription on the Jin Shrine' ('Jinsi bei'), composed by Taizong when he visited his family's ancestral temple in Taiyuan; and the newly compiled *History of the Jin* (*Jin shu*), a history of the Jin dynasty (265–420) compiled by Fang Xuanling (578–648) and other members of the Tang historiography bureau in 644. In 686 Silla king Sinmun dispatched emissaries to present a memorial to the throne requesting the *Rites of Tang* (*Tang li*) and other writings. Empress Dowager Wu Zetian (Wu Zhao) gifted them with the *Essential Rites on Auspiciousness and Inauspiciousness* (*Jixiong yaoli*) and the 'Admonitions' ('Guijie') section from the *Forest of Fine Phrases from the Literary Institute* (*Wenguan cilin*); she also insisted that a complete set in fifty rolls be bestowed on the Silla emissaries. These writings likely served as literary models for young student scholars to emulate.

In 717 Silla king Sŏngdŏk sent the noble Kim Such'ung as an emissary to Tang. He was gifted with portraits of Confucius, the 10 philosophers and 72 disciples, which were enshrined in Silla's State Academy. By installing these portraits, Silla could now convene its own commemoration rituals for Confucius, which suggests that Silla writers' skills in literary Sinitic composition had advanced appreciably. This is because the formally sanctioned litanies read and ceremonially burned during these official sacrifices needed to be composed in literary Sinitic according to rigorous standards. Extant examples of Silla epigraphy from the early eighth century, such as the inscription on the gilt-bronze *śarīra* container excavated from Hwangbok Monastery (706) and the inscriptions on the standing stone Buddhist images of Maitreya and Amitābha at Kamsan Monastery (719), demonstrate the enhanced quality of literary composition in Silla when contrasted with prior epigraphic evidence from the sixth and seventh centuries.

Confucian Mores in Biographical Narratives

Conventional accounts of Confucianism in the Greater Silla period are centred on biographical narratives of loyal officials preserved in the *History of the Three Kingdoms*. Before turning to these seminal figures, however, I would draw attention to another body of popular tales preserved in this twelfth-century work: narratives heralding filial sons, dutiful daughters, chaste wives and loyal subjects. Numerous narratives of this sort circulated widely in medieval China both verbally and in written form, serving to promote and popularize 'Confucian' social practices. However, as we have seen above in a few Buddhist-inspired tales, there were no clear lines between Buddhist and Confucian morality. In reality, as stories of these kinds spread to Korea, Japan and Vietnam, they contributed to the creation of the mainstream Sinitic social culture shared throughout East Asia. For the case of Silla, Kim Pusik's

Figurine of Silla woman, from old tomb in Hwangsŏng-dong, Kyŏngju, 7th century CE, clay.

work preserves examples of such tales, which served as evidence of Silla's civilized status as a 'country of Confucian gentlemen'. Here I will summarize a few stories illustrating the core Confucian values of female faithfulness and filial piety, and then present biographies of Silla's great Confucian scholar-officials, which highlight aspects of respectable behaviour.

Miss Sŏl was a girl from a poor commoner family living in Chestnut Village during the reign of King Chinp'yŏng (579–632). She was beautiful and had a cheerful countenance and personality. Her father was already old when a draft call came to protect the frontier from enemy incursions. Unlike Mulan in the well-known Chinese tale, Miss Sŏl was unable to take her father's place. A young man named Kasil from the Saryang region of Silla had always liked Miss Sŏl and offered to fulfil her father's obligation of military service if she would marry him. Kasil and Miss Sŏl's father agreed that the marriage would take place when he returned from his three-year term of duty. They took a mirror, broke it in half, and each took a piece. Because of Silla's dire circumstances, men posted to the frontiers were not allowed to return home – and Kasil was gone for more than six years. Believing he was dead, Miss Sŏl's father continually pressured her to marry somebody else. Miss Sŏl chastised her father saying, 'If we abandon our trust and break our promise, how can we claim to possess human emotions? In the end I do not dare follow your command, father. Please do not speak to me about this again.' Despite her plea, her old father planned to force her to marry someone in the village. Miss Sŏl firmly refused him and planned to run away. Hiding in the barn, she looked at the horse Kasil had left behind and her half-piece of mirror. Eventually an emaciated Kasil in ragged clothes returned from military service. Nobody recognized him, but he produced his piece of broken mirror. Sobbing, Miss Sŏl picked it up, and everyone in the village was overjoyed. They were subsequently married and lived to a ripe old age together.

Chiŭn was the daughter of the commoner Yŏn'gwan in the Han'gi region of the Silla capital. Her father died when she was young and, refusing marriage, she worked hard to support her widowed mother. If she had no food to feed her, she sometimes worked as a hired labourer or domestic help, and sometimes she went begging to obtain food. She eventually sold herself as a slave to a wealthy household for ten piculs of rice. After four days of eating the pleasant-tasting rice, Chiŭn's mother realized that her daughter had sold herself into slavery and, bursting into tears, lamented that she had not died quickly and had burdened her daughter. The *hwarang* Hyojong witnessed this drama and requested that his noble parents donate a hundred piculs of millet and clothing to Chiŭn's family. Hyojong purchased her freedom, and each of his followers donated one picul of millet. When Silla king Chŏnggang (r. 886–7) heard the story, he bestowed on the women five hundred piculs of tax rice and a house and exempted them from compulsory corvée labour. Because they had so much millet, the king feared that people would steal from them, so he commanded the local authorities to send troops to guard them in shifts. In addition, the king renamed the village the 'Precinct of Filial Devotion', and sent a memorial to Tang documenting the story. The Tang imperial court collected stories of these kinds because outstanding moral behaviour by the common people served as evidence of the dynasty's possessing the Mandate of Heaven.

Kangsu (d. *c.* 681–92), whose family of Kaya heritage had moved from the Saryang region of the capital to the Chungwŏn Minor Capital (present-day Ch'ungju in North Ch'ungch'ŏng province), was a master of the refined literature of the time. Possessing skills in literary composition, he drafted memorials for kings Muyŏl and Munmu in the seventh century. From his youth, he had an ongoing relationship with the daughter of a blacksmith, who scholars believe may have lived in the nearby village of Pugok (present-day Chech'ŏn). Although his parents sought to marry their talented son to a daughter of a more illustrious house, Kangsu, who loved his simple, common-law wife, bowed twice to his father and replied, paraphrasing a famous line from the 'Biography of Song Hong' from the *History of Later Han*:

> To be poor and humble is not something to be ashamed of. To study the Way and not practise it is truly something to be ashamed of. I previously heard that the ancients said, 'A wife married in times of poverty must not be set aside. Relations

> formed when one is poor and humble ought not to be forgotten.' This being the case, I cannot bear to abandon my lowborn wife.

Sŏl Ch'ong (*c*. 660–730) was the head-rank six son of the monk Wŏnhyo and a widowed Silla princess. He read the nine classics using the Silla vernacular and instructed the rising generation of scholar-officials. Sŏl Ch'ong was considered the 'ancestor' of Confucian scholars in Korea from the Koryŏ period, if not earlier. His biography preserves a politically oriented allegory on seeking wise counsel at court presented to Silla king Sinmun on a balmy midsummer evening. The 'Parable of the Flower King' recounts how the King of Flowers, the Peony, came to this land, established court and flourished. Then luscious and attractive spirits, tender and young flowers, rushed to present themselves before him. First, an incomparably beautiful woman, Wild Rose, offered her services to the Flower King. After that, a withered old man, the White Pasque Flower, offered his experience and down-to-earth sensibilities so that the king could endure well the vicissitudes of life and want. Because the Flower King hankered for the sensuous beauty of Wild Rose and did not recognize the intrinsic worth of the White Pasque Flower, the old man chastised him,

> I came here because I heard the king was clever and recognized reason. Now I see I was wrong. Generally, those who are lords usually become intimate with the villainous and flatterers and commonly estrange the honest and upright. For this reason, Mencius [Meng Ke] did not encounter such a ruler to the end of his life. Feng Tang [*fl*. 180–141 BCE, a minister of the ancient Han dynasty who dared to criticize the emperor for employing incompetent men in high positions] was a lowly gentleman of the interior in hiding until his hair turned white. Because it has been thus since antiquity, what can I do?

King Sinmun grasped Sŏl Ch'ong's meaning, had him commit the allegory to writing to educate future generations and promoted him to a lofty position.

Tomb of Sŏl Ch'ong, Kyŏngju, 8th century CE.

Nokchin (*fl.* 818–22) was a head-rank six elite serving in the Silla bureaucracy. Senior Grand Councillor Ch'unggong had worried himself sick in the Administration Chamber over the problems managing the government and, especially, selecting appropriate officials at court. The king told him to rest and take medicine for a few days. Nokchin visited him at his home and gave him the following sage advice and honest assessment of the problems faced by the Silla government:

> When a carpenter builds a home, large pieces of lumber are used for roof beams and pillars, and small ones for rafters. Once crooked and straight pieces are each placed in secure places, then will a great mansion be completed. Since antiquity, has governing by means of worthy grand councillors ever been different? If you place men of immense talent in high positions and men of lesser talent in lower positions, the six ministries and hundred officials at court down to provincial earls, aggregation leaders, commandery governors and district magistrates, no position will be unfilled at court and every position will be filled by a qualified person. There will be order between high

> and low, and the worthy and unworthy will be differentiated. Only then will the royal administration be complete. At present, however, this is not the case. Nepotism destroys the common good, and official positions are selected for men. If one is in favour, even though he is incompetent, he is judged worthy and presented with a high position in the royal court. If one is in disfavour, even though he is capable, traps are set for him and he is stuck in a deep ditch. If, in accepting and rejecting a course of action, muddled are your thoughts, and if in distinguishing between right and wrong, chaotic are your intentions, not only will affairs of state be turbid and disorderly, but those who do them will also be exhausted and ill. If those entrusted with official positions are pure and white, they will attend to affairs scrupulously and respectfully, prevent the approach of bribery and distance themselves from implications in special petitions. Promotion and demotion should only depend on one's relative intelligence and giving and taking should not depend on whether one is in favour or disfavour, just like a scale must not be crooked to measure whether something is light or heavy, and just like a plumb line must not be warped to indicate whether something is crooked or straight. If this is so, the administration of punishments will be just and solemn, and the state will be peaceful.[13]

Nokchin's words were like a medicinal tonic to Ch'unggong, who returned to work re-energized and recommitted to finding well-qualified people to serve in government. Although King Hŏndŏk (r. 809–26) sought to raise Nokchin to the capital rank of *taeach'an* (rank 5) after he rendered loyal service to the throne during the Kim Hŏnch'ang rebellion of 822, he politely declined the honour.

Ch'oe Ch'iwŏn (857–after 908), a talented poet and scholar-official, was from the Saryang region of the Silla capital, according to his biography in the *History of the Three Kingdoms*. Like Sŏl Ch'ong and Nokchin, he was also a head-rank six elite in Silla's highly stratified social order. He was born during the waning years of Silla's hegemony over the Korean peninsula, and his birth status disqualified him from obtaining a high post in Silla's government.

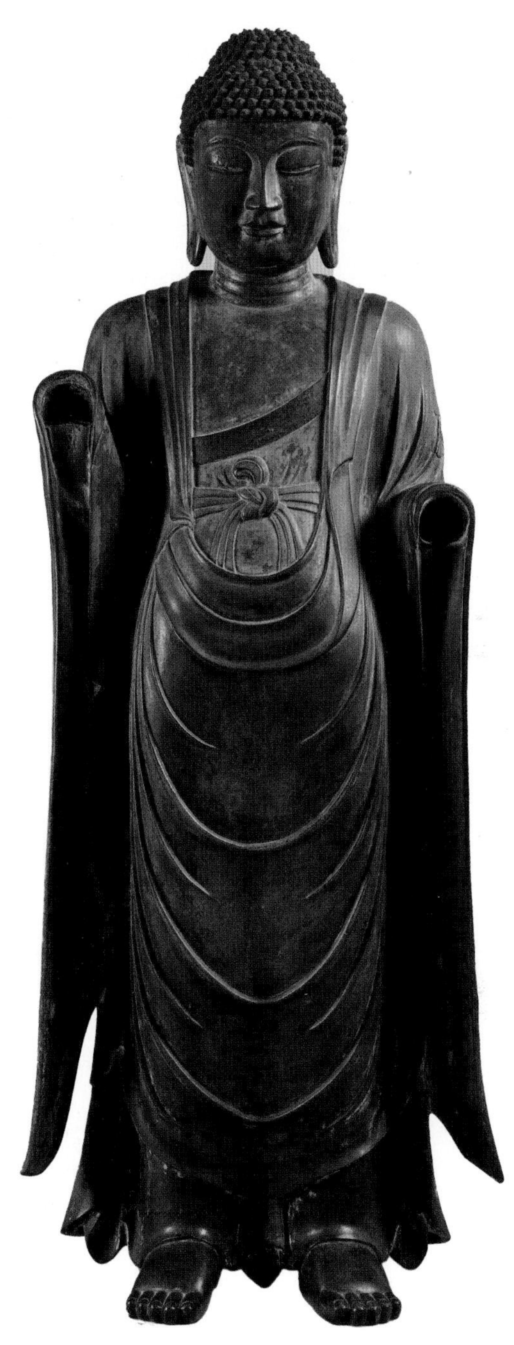

Standing Bhaiṣajyaguru, from site of Paengnyul Monastery, Kyŏngju, 8th century CE.

In 868 his father sent him to study in Tang China at the young age of twelve, saying, 'If you do not pass the imperial examination within ten years, you are not my son. Go and exert yourself towards it.' Upon arriving in Tang, he studied diligently under his mentor Pei Zan (dates unknown), Attendant Gentleman of the Ministry of Rites, and passed the imperial examination in 874. After first serving as a district defender south of the Yangzi river, he became famous for composing admonitory letters sent to the rebel leader Huang Chao (835–884), leading to a brief but illustrious career in the sprawling Tang civil and military bureaucracy. His collected works, *Plowing a Cinnamon Garden with a Writing Brush* (*Kyewŏn p'ilgyŏng*), and other works in parallel prose are mentioned in the monograph on literature in the *New History of the Tang*.

Because he desired to return to his homeland, Tang emperor Xizong (r. 874–88) sent him to Silla bearing an imperial edict in 885. Despite serving in a series of positions in Silla's court, such as Attendant Reader, Hallim Academician, Attendant Gentleman of the Board of War and Director of Administrative Scribes, he was never placed in a position with enough power to implement the reforms he deemed were essential to renovate and invigorate the declining Silla government. In the spring of 894 he presented a ten-point memorial on current affairs to Queen Chinsŏng (r. 887–97). Although she received it with gladness and advanced Ch'oe to the rank of *ach'an* (rank 6), the highest capital rank possible for a head-rank six elite, none of his reform measures were acted upon. The primary reason for the failure of Ch'oe Ch'iwŏn's reforms was that the true-bone nobles monopolized all positions of actual political power in Silla and discriminated against their lower-ranking countrymen, in spite of (and probably due to) the fact that the latter were well educated. In other words, Ch'oe's fame in Tang was likely threatening to the nobles in power; so, although they favoured him with some respect, they placed him in no position to make reforms that would endanger their hold over the country. After his failure to promote change in the capital, Ch'oe was dispatched to a few provincial posts. Discouraged and appalled by the ossification of Silla government, Ch'oe reportedly made arcane books his bedmates and wrote erotic poetry (*p'ungwŏl*, 'wind and moonlight music') while visiting mountains and monasteries throughout the country. He ultimately sought reclusion at Haein Monastery, in the north of present-day South Kyŏngsang province, where he secretly resided with his mother's older brothers, who were both Buddhist monks. Ch'oe is said to have pursued the path to enlightenment with them until he passed away at an old age. Ch'oe's official biography asserts that he recognized the potential of Wang Kŏn (877–943), the founder of the succeeding Koryŏ dynasty, early in Wang's career as a general under Kungye (*fl.* 891–918), and that Ch'oe's disciples sought an audience with him to offer their services to the fledgling Koryŏ state. In 1020 Ch'oe was posthumously granted the lofty title of secretariat director, a position similar to a grand councillor who consulted with the ruler on major governmental positions, by Koryŏ king Hyŏnjong (r. 1009–31).

Figurine of Silla official, Kyŏngju, 8th century CE, clay.

SEVEN

The Good, the Bad and the Ugly in the Later Three Kingdoms

The prestige and authority of the Silla ruling family fell and rose repeatedly over the period stretching from the late eighth century to the end of the ninth century. True-bone nobles serving the Silla state and related to Kim Ch'unch'u's direct line of descendants who sat on the Silla throne between 654 and 780 killed the hapless young King Hyegong (r. 765–80) and then competed among themselves for the throne over the course of the ninth century. Several *coups d'ètat* resulted in regicide. Rebellions and revolts among nobles in branches of the Kim lineage claiming descent from the most-likely legendary King Naemul (traditionally r. 356–402) arose regularly, and the highest-ranking true-bone nobles monopolized the highest positions at court. On top of this, drought, famine and pestilence recurred with increasing frequency over the course of the ninth century, making the lives of common people miserable and leading many to surrender themselves as slaves to more wealthy lords in possession of manors and to large landowning Buddhist monasteries. Although the ultimate result was the inexorable decline of the state's fortunes and of control over its peninsular domain, that Silla would falter did not seem a foregone conclusion to many elites who served in its government in the late ninth century. The reasons for Silla's decline may be summarized as follows: Silla's ruling structure had lost the flexibility of the late seventh and early eighth centuries and had ossified due to unilateral control by true-bone nobles. In addition, repeated failed harvests and difficulties among the common people bore the bitter fruit of banditry and rebellion in the remote prefectures in the north and southwest. The historical memory of the major players in the Later Three Kingdoms period may be likened to the characters in the famous spaghetti western *The Good, the Bad and the Ugly*, following the title of an essay by G. Cameron Hurst (published in 1981). After describing the decline of Silla and the origin of the Later Three Kingdoms period, we will briefly examine in turn 'the Ugly', Later Koguryŏ's Kungye (*fl.* 891–918); 'the Bad', Later Paekche's Kyŏn Hwŏn (*fl.* 892–936); and 'the Good', Koryŏ's Wang Kŏn (877–943).

Queen Chinsŏng and the Decline of Silla

Korean scholarship, following Kim Pusik's *History of the Three Kingdoms*, has conventionally blamed the demise of the dynasty on Queen Chindŏk (r. 887–97), the last of three queens to rule Silla. To understand why this blame is misplaced, we must return to the reign of her father, King Kyŏngmun (r. 861–75), and begin with one of the most entertaining and instructive narratives of the late Silla period. In 860, before Kyŏngmun ascended the throne, he was a fifteen-year-old *hwarang* named Kim Ŭngnyŏm, a grandson of the short-reigned King Hŭigang (r. 836–8), who had committed suicide after a palace coup attempt on his life. When, from his travels among the common people all over the country, the young man reported signs of the king's good and humane rule, King Hŏnan (r. 857–61) was so pleased and impressed with him that he offered him the hand in marriage of one of his two daughters. Hŏnan's twenty-year-old elder daughter was plain-looking, but the nineteen-year-old younger daughter was attractive. Ŭngnyŏm's mother strongly encouraged him to marry the younger daughter, but the Buddhist monk Pŏmgyo, who was the head of the *hwarang*'s followers and functioned rather like a spiritual adviser, informed him that if he chose the younger daughter the monk would die in his presence, but if he married the elder daughter three good things would happen. Ŭngnyŏm decided to follow the monk's advice and wedded the elder daughter. The three good things were that he made his royal parents-in-law happy, he was made heir apparent by the king because the king had no sons, and after ascending the throne in 861 he was free to make the beautiful younger daughter a consort.

Ŭngnyŏm's younger brother Kim Wihong (d. 888) was probably born before 850. His ill-starred grandfather's difficulties in holding the Silla throne, in conjunction with the plotting and strategic manoeuvres of his relatives, would not have been forgotten by Wihong as he amassed authority and influence during the reign of his brother. Extant epigraphy shows that Wihong became the most powerful true-bone noble in Silla from at least the early 870s. He held sway over Silla's government as grand councillor, the dominant member of the Administration Chamber, supporting his brother through the crafting of policy. When his nephew King Hŏn'gang (r. 875–86) ascended the throne in 875, Wihong also became the senior grandee, responsible for supervising transitions of royal power. Wihong continued serving as both senior grand councillor and senior grandee through the unexpectedly short reign of King Chŏnggang (r. 886–7), Hŏn'gang's younger brother, and into the beginning of the reign of Queen Chinsŏng. King Hŏn'gang had a son named Yo who was less than a year old when his father died, but the unanticipated passing of King Chŏnggang caused their younger sister Chinsŏng, who was likely born in about 865, to be raised to the throne.

The Silla annals preserved in the *History of the Three Kingdoms* provide concise information demonstrating that Silla monarchs attempted to lead their country through a constant barrage of epidemics, floods, droughts and earthquakes during the mid- to late ninth century. In Chinese-style historiography inspired by Confucianism, natural calamities of these kinds are conventionally understood as evidence that the ruling dynasty's mandate to rule is wavering. These vexing circumstances also helped others conspiring to rebel against Silla rule by drawing disgruntled and suffering individuals to their causes. King Kyŏngmun's reign was marked by a litany of disasters. A plague struck the capital in 867 and a flood caused devasting crop failure. An earthquake, flood and plague afflicted Silla in 870. No snow fell in the winter of that year, adding to the bitter conditions being endured by the farming

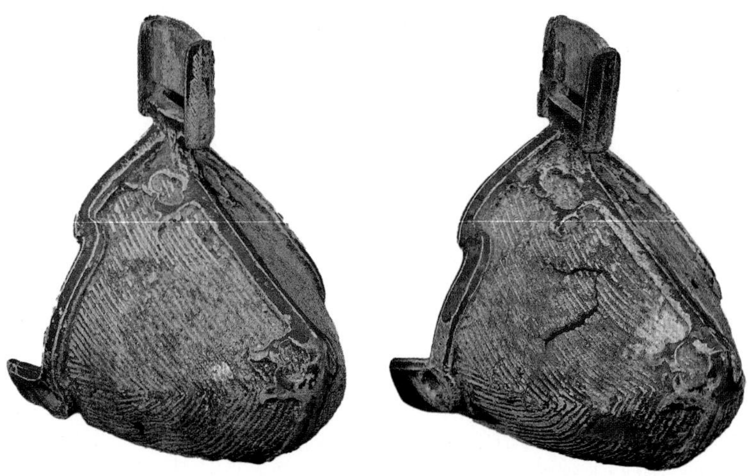

Lacquered stirrups, Greater Silla, 9th–10th century CE, cast iron with coloured inlay.

population. Another earthquake stuck Silla in 872, and the common people starved in 873, which contributed to another epidemic. The *ich'an* (rank 2) Kŭnjong conspired to rebel and attempted a palace coup, but it failed, and he and his co-conspirators were executed. Although Kŭnjong is not mentioned elsewhere in the *History of the Three Kingdoms*, his holding the high rank of *ich'an* is evidence that he was a true-bone noble and probably related to the royal Kim family. The *ilgilch'an* (rank 7) Sinhong rebelled in the summer of 879, during the reign of Hŏn'gang, but he was apprehended and killed. The *ich'an* (rank 2) Kim Yo of Hanju rebelled in the spring of 887, during the short reign of Chŏnggang, but the Silla court was able to suppress the revolt by sending troops north in a timely manner. Hanju was Silla's northwestern prefecture, covering present-day Kyŏnggi province, with large holdings in the modern Kangwŏn and North Ch'ungch'ŏng provinces. This prefecture controlled the relatively productive agricultural land in the Han river basin near present-day Seoul as well as modern-day Kaesŏng, the region from which the Koryŏ founder Wang Kŏn hailed. Kim Yo was also likely a member of the extended Silla royal family.

King Chŏnggang was only in his twenties when he passed away after less than a year on the throne. Kim Wihong was in his mid- to late thirties and at the pinnacle of power in Silla when his niece

Chinsŏng assumed the throne. Although Wihong was married to a court lady, he had regularly engaged in intimate sexual relations with Chinsŏng ever since her youth and frequently entered the palace to carry out business. In essence he had cemented his control over the royal family through his relationships, and Queen Chinsŏng was so devoted to him that she posthumously awarded her paramour the regnal title Great King Hyesŏng after his sudden and unexpected death. Both the *History of the Three Kingdoms* and the *Memorabilia of the Three Kingdoms* report flattery and political chaos and confusion in Chinsŏng's court both before and after the passing of Wihong, and, following Kim Pusik, most historians have traditionally criticized Chinsŏng for the rapid demise of Silla. This verdict seems oddly inadequate and lopsided considering the pervasive problems within Silla's government caused by the true-bone nobles dominating all the highest-level positions and their persistent quarrelling and intrigues. Just as important, Chinsŏng was never intended to assume the throne, and her government was dominated by Wihong prior to his passing.

Drought conditions returned in the summer of 888, making matters worse for the young queen, who had fallen seriously ill in

Tomb of Silla king Hŭngdŏk (r. 825–36), Kyŏngju.

the third lunar month of that year. The *History of the Three Kingdoms* reports that Chinsŏng's sickness only cleared up after she pardoned guilty prisoners from the death sentence and allowed sixty prospective men to become monks. In 889, most likely because of the previous year's drought, the prefectures and commanderies did not dispatch their taxes, which were assessed in rice and grain, to the capital. Although she had attempted to assuage the people the previous year, Chinsŏng was forced to send commissioners to enforce tax collection because the state's storehouses were empty. Her decision to collect taxes in these trying circumstances gave rise to banditry in the far-flung regions of Silla. Even prefectural officials or local true-bone nobles were incited to revolt, the most important being Wŏnjong and Aeno, who were based in Sabŏlchu, present-day Sangju in North Kyŏngsang province. Since Sabŏlchu was the prefectural seat of Sangju and located close to Silla's capital region, Yangju, Chinsŏng had to quell this rebellion before it spread to the Silla heartland. She was able to do so with the assistance of a local village chief, but uprisings and banditry in more remote regions were difficult to control due to Silla's increasingly limited resources.

The Emergence of Kungye and Kyŏn Hwŏn

In 891 the bandit leader Yanggil took control of Silla's northern minor capital, Pugwŏn, and dispatched his deputy, Kungye, leading more than a hundred horsemen, to assault settlements loyal to Silla to the east of Pugwŏn in the north-central prefecture of Sakchu and districts under the control of the northeastern prefecture of Myŏngju in modern Kangwŏn province. In time, Yanggil held sway over Silla's Sakchu, Sangju and Myŏngju prefectures. The following year, 892, Kyŏn Hwŏn proclaimed the establishment of his own Later Paekche kingdom from his seat of power in Wansanju, present-day Chŏnju, in Silla's west-central prefecture. The *History of the Three Kingdoms* reports that Kyŏn Hwŏn was a farmer's son from Kaŭn District in Sangju and was originally surnamed Yi. He adopted the surname Kyŏn when he actively began attempting to re-establish Paekche and overthrow Silla. After he subdued the commanderies and districts in Silla's southeastern prefecture of Muju, the territory under Kyŏn Hwŏn's uncontested control roughly comprised the regions of modern North and South Chŏlla provinces.

Kungye's origins are debated by scholars; however, the general consensus is that he was most likely an 'illegitimate' Silla prince, the son of King Hŏnan with a concubine of low birth, and hence not possessing true-bone status. The *History of the Three Kingdoms* records what may be later legends that inauspicious omens connected with Kungye's birth caused the Silla king to order a courtier to kill him by throwing him down some stairs; he was reportedly saved by a wet nurse who raised him in secret. We may never know whether these are true, but they do make a dramatic story. Kungye spent some time as a monk in Silla's northeastern prefecture of Myŏngju, and then he joined Yanggil's bandit group. By the end of 894 Kungye was preparing to establish himself as a rebel leader separate from Yanggil. He struck out eastward with six hundred loyal followers, entering Hasŭlla, modern Kangnŭng, in Myŏngju, and took the title 'general'. After further strengthening his mobile army, he advanced westward during the autumn of 895 and subjugated Silla commanderies as he progressed. He destroyed the Silla forces defending Puyak and Ch'ŏrwŏn and gained control of more than ten commanderies and districts previously under the jurisdiction of Silla's northwestern prefecture, Hanju. Kungye's break with Yanggil seems to have occurred at this time, and his biography in the *History of the Three Kingdoms* says that Kungye now started to style himself 'king' because the land under his direct control was large enough to constitute a kingdom. Since the extant sources do not say what he called his newly formed state, scholars have conventionally used the term 'Later Koguryŏ' to refer to Kungye's domain. In 896 Wang Kŏn, whose family stronghold was in Songak (modern Kaesŏng), became a subject of Kungye and was awarded the position of grand protector (military governor) of Ch'ŏrwŏn commandery by Kungye. Kungye eventually made Ch'ŏrwŏn his capital after using Songak in this capacity for a brief period of time.

The Silla annals report that outlaws became prominent in Silla's southwestern region in 896, the tenth year of Queen Chinsŏng's reign. The extremely concise account does not explain whether they

Vajradhara, Buddhist guardians, Hadong, Kyŏngju, 9th century CE.

were affiliated with Kyŏn Hwŏn's Later Paekche or whether 'south-western' now referred to Silla's prefecture of Kangju, based in modern Chinju in South Kyŏngsang province. The people called them the 'red-trouser bandits' because members of the group wore red trousers to differentiate themselves from government troops. Travelling eastward, these new bandits ransacked the prefectures and commanderies they encountered and raided as far as Moryang village to the west of the Silla capital. After looting people's homes in Moryang village, they abruptly returned westward. Because the common people and farmers were devastated and brigands were in abundance, Queen Chinsŏng officially announced her intention to abdicate the throne to her young nephew Kim Yo (b. *c.* 886), King Hŏn'gang's son, the following summer, in 897.

The reigns of Silla's last five rulers, kings Hyogong (897–912), Sindŏk (912–17), Kyŏngmyŏng (917–24), Kyŏngae (924–7) and

Kyŏngsun (927–35), mark the steady decline of Silla's territory. Silla was reduced to the territory immediately surrounding the capital region due to the methodical acquisition of land by Kyŏn Hwŏn, Kungye and Kungye's subordinate and successor, Wang Kŏn (877–943, Koryŏ king T'aejo, r. 918–43). The *History of the Three Kingdoms* and the *Memorabilia of the Three Kingdoms* assert that three of these last five rulers were surnamed Pak rather than Kim; however, a closer examination of their genealogies shows that they were actually surnamed Kim. The claim that these rulers were surnamed Pak likely functioned as a means to support the dynastic transition to the Wang family of Koryŏ, just as the assertion that the Chinese emperor Qin Shihuang (Ying Zheng, r. 221–210 BCE) was really the son of the wealthy merchant and courtier Lü Buwei (291–235 BCE) facilitated the establishment of the Han dynasty (206 BCE–220 CE), and the claim that Koryŏ kings U (r. 1374–88) and Ch'ang (r. 1388–9) were not really sons of King Kongmin (r. 1351–74) but actually the progeny of the monk Sindon (1322–1371) supported the founding of the Chosŏn dynasty (1392–1910).

Kungye laid claim to P'aesŏ circuit and more than thirty fortresses under the control of Silla's Hansan prefecture during the reign of King Hyogong. He made Songak commandery his capital in 898. Once Kungye officially declared Songak his capital, Yanggil became worried that he would double-cross him. Yanggil and his bandit group plotted to assault Kungye in 899; however, they were routed, and Yanggil ceased to be a contender for power in the northern border areas of Silla. Many of Yanggil's leaders became Kungye's subordinates in 900, and Kungye publicly declared himself 'king' in 901. Kyŏn Hwŏn assaulted Taeya Fortress, modern Hapch'ŏn in South Kyŏngsang province, in the autumn of 901, but failed to take it. Nevertheless, he pillaged settlements south of the borders of Kŭmsŏng, modern Naju in South Chŏlla province, on his return. In 904 Kungye instituted government offices similar to those of Silla and named his country Majin, which is an abbreviated transliteration of 'Mahācīnasthāna', suggesting that Kungye imagined himself as establishing a state with the symbolic potential to rival China. During this time, districts in Silla's northern prefectures continually yielded to Kungye. In 905 Kungye moved his

Stele of eminent Silla monk Zen master Wŏllang (Taet'ong, 813–883), late 9th century CE.

capital to the more central location of Ch'ŏrwŏn so that he could concentrate his efforts on subjugating Chungnyŏng ('bamboo pass'), a strategic corridor adjoining modern North Ch'ungch'ŏng province and North Kyŏngsang province. Kyŏn Hwŏn claimed ten commanderies south of Silla's Ilsŏn commandery, modern Sŏnsan in North Kyŏngsang province, in 907. Kungye made his first assault against Kyŏn Hwŏn's territory in 909, by dispatching a naval force to conquer Chindo commandery, the stronghold controlling this large island on the southwestern extremity of the Korean peninsula. In 910 Kyŏn Hwŏn laid siege to Naju Fortress for ten days, supported by a large force of cavalry and infantry, and only retreated when Kungye dispatched his navy to attack. Kyŏn Hwŏn laid siege to Taeya Fortress again in 916, but failed to subdue it. In the second month of 918, just a few months after being enthroned, Silla king Kyŏngmyŏng quashed the *ilgilch'an* (rank 7) Hyŏnsŏng's revolt.

Kungye, 'the Ugly'

In 911 Kungye changed the name of his state to T'aebong (meaning 'enfeoffed of/on Mount Tai', China's sacred marchmount of the east), which seems to claim that heaven sanctioned his rule and would bestow peace and prosperity. Soon thereafter he proclaimed himself to be the future Buddha Maitreya (*Mirŭk pul*) and named his sons the bodhisattvas Green Light (*Ch'ŏnggwang posal*) and Divine Light (*Sin'gwang posal*). Kungye wore a peaked gold hood on his head and a square robe on his body like a monk, and when he went out he always rode a white horse whose mane and tail were adorned with silk ornaments. Mimicking Buddhist ritual processions, he had young boys and girls lead the way before him carrying banners and parasols, purifying the air with incense and flowers. He also had more than two hundred Buddhist monks follow his train chanting Buddhist hymns in Sanskrit (*pŏmp'ae*). Kungye is also said to have composed more than twenty rolls of Buddhist scriptures. The authenticity of these works was denounced by the monk Sŏkch'ong, but he was bludgeoned to death with an iron mallet for it.

In 918, when Kungye's wife Lady Kang reprimanded him for this behaviour, he accused her of illicit relations with other men, declaring that he knew this through his supernormal power, which he termed 'Maitreya's method of observing the mind' (*Mirŭk kwansim pŏp*). As a result, in his rage he killed his wife by inserting a burning hot iron rod into her womb, and he also slew their sons. This was the last straw for his comrades-in-arms, who had observed his suspicions and wanton treachery towards his subordinates steadily increase. Kungye's followers then convinced Wang Kŏn, Kungye's most successful general, to become their new king and rose in revolt in the summer of 918. Kungye fled his capital in disguise but was later killed by the people of Puyang, modern Pyŏnggang in Kangwŏn province, one of the areas that suffered the most due to Kungye's excesses.

Kyŏn Hwŏn, 'the Bad'

In the tenth month of 920, Kyŏn Hwŏn attacked Taeya Fortress for the third time, with a large force of cavalry and infantry, and finally succeeded in subduing it. He continued his offensive southward and planned to lay siege to Chillye Fortress, near modern Ch'angwŏn or Kimhae in South Kyŏngsang province. Silla king Kyŏngmyŏng quickly sent an emissary to Wang Kŏn, begging for Koryŏ's assistance. Apprised of Silla's call for help, Kyŏn Hwŏn abandoned his military initiative. Kyŏn Hwŏn's territorial expansion floundered in the mid-920s, and he attempted to slow the advance of Koryŏ by sending his nephew, Chinho, to the Koryŏ capital as a hostage in

Roof tiles with dragon face, Greater Silla, Kyŏngju, 8th–9th century, earthenware.

the eleventh month of 925. The newly enthroned Silla king Kyŏngae sent an emissary to Wang Kŏn warning him to be wary of Kyŏn Hwŏn's machinations and not to trust him. The hostage Chinho died suddenly in Koryŏ in the fourth month of 926, however, and Kyŏn Hwŏn believed that Wang Kŏn had intentionally killed him. Kyŏn Hwŏn ordered the mobilization of Later Paekche's forces for a punitive expedition against Koryŏ. Wang Kŏn admonished his generals to persevere and withstand attempts at sieges of their fortresses and strongholds. After the Later Paekche invasion stalled, Wang Kŏn went on the offensive, and Silla sent troops to support him in the first month of 927.

Seeking to exact revenge on Silla for its support of Koryŏ's incursion, Kyŏn Hwŏn attacked Silla's border force at Koul superior prefecture in the ninth month of 927. Silla plied Koryŏ for military aid, but relief did not reach Silla in time to safeguard the Silla capital from a devastating invasion in the eleventh month. The lightning attack on the Silla capital caught the Silla king and queen by surprise while they were enjoying a feast at P'osŏk Pavilion, a circular arrangement of specially carved stones in the shape of an abalone, around which wine cups could be floated without the contents spilling. While the royal party sought refuge in the rear palace, many members of the Silla court were captured as they attempted to flee in various directions. Kyŏn Hwŏn qualifies as 'the Bad' for the following reasons. He permitted his subordinate troops to loot the Silla capital at will. He had the Silla king, his consort and several concubines withdrawn from the rear palace and dispatched to his military camps. He forced King Kyŏngae to commit suicide and raped his primary consort, and he permitted his underlings to sexually assault the royal concubines. Finally, Kyŏn Hwŏn tried to break the Silla–Koryŏ alliance by enthroning the king's brother, Kim Pu (d. 978), who would be remembered as King Kyŏngsun. To cause further havoc and difficulty for Silla, Kyŏn Hwŏn had his forces raid Taemok commandery, modern Ch'ilgok in North Kyŏngsang province, and burn the fields and the grain stored out in the open on the fields in the twelfth month of 927.

The Silla general guarding Kangju yielded to Kyŏn Hwŏn in 928, and Later Paekche attempted to secure more territory by erecting a fortress at Yangsan, modern Yŏngdong in North Ch'ungch'ŏng province. Wang Kŏn charged the general of Myŏngji Fortress to assault them while the stronghold was under construction. Camping below Taeya Fortress, Kyŏn Hwŏn dispatched auxiliaries to commandeer Taemok commandery's remaining crops in the eighth month. He captured Mugok Fortress, modern Kunwi in North Kyŏngsang province, in the tenth month. Attempting to break the alliance between Koryŏ and Silla, the king of Later Paekche continued to attack Silla strongholds, such as Ŭisŏng superior prefecture, modern Ŭisŏng in North Kyŏngsang province, in 929. Although Wang Kŏn attempted to support Silla by sending some of his most skilled generals, they were killed or surrendered to Later Paekche forces. Basking in his success, Kyŏn Hwŏn attempted

P'osŏk Pavilion Site, Namsan, Kyŏngju.

to surround Kaŭn district in Silla's Sangju, but he was unable to subdue it and was forced to withdraw.

Kyŏn Hwŏn married many women and had more than ten sons. Because his fourth son, Kŭmgang, was particularly tall and intelligent, Kyŏn Hwŏn seemed to favour him over his three elder brothers, Sin'gŏm, Yanggŏm and Yonggŏm. The *ich'an* Nŭnghwan instigated a plot with Yanggŏm and others to execute a coup to overthrow Kyŏn Hwŏn and place Sin'gŏm on the throne. In 935 Yanggŏm and Yonggŏm, who were serving as governors of prefectures away from the capital, convinced Sin'gŏm to imprison their father and have Kŭmgang killed. Sin'gŏm then declared himself king of Later Paekche. Kyŏn Hwŏn was held prisoner at Kŭmsan Monastery for three months, but in the sixth month he escaped to Kŭmsŏng (modern Naju) with another son and one of his concubines. Eventually Kyŏn Hwŏn made his way to Wang Kŏn's court, submitted himself to him, and appealed to the Koryŏ king to punish his traitorous sons. Although Sin'gŏm marshalled the Paekche forces, they were ultimately overwhelmed by Koryŏ troops and surrendered to Wang Kŏn. Nŭnghwan, Yanggŏm and Yonggŏm were executed, but, on Nŭnghwan's testimony, because Sin'gŏm was coerced to dethrone his father and did not bear malice towards him in his heart, his sentence was commuted. Kyŏn Hwŏn died the following year, 936, after developing a large tumour on his back. In this way, Later Paekche ended and was absorbed into Koryŏ in 935.

Wang Kŏn, 'the Good'

The *History of the Three Kingdoms* and the *History of Koryŏ* (*Koryŏsa*) depict Wang Kŏn as the consummate and humane protector of Silla. For this reason, 'the good' Koryŏ king ultimately received the Mandate of Heaven to reunite the Three Kingdoms. In the summer of 918, after replacing Kungye and renaming the state 'Koryŏ', Wang Kŏn moved his capital to Songak (Kaesŏng). Kyŏngmyŏng and Wang Kŏn exchanged ambassadors and signed a peace treaty, promising mutual aid against Kyŏn Hwŏn. The Silla annals report that Silla dispatched an envoy named Kim Yul to the Koryŏ capital to meet the Koryŏ king. He returned to Silla with his report in the first month of 921. He said that the Koryŏ king asked about Silla's three treasures: the 5-metre (16 ft) statue of the Buddha and nine-storey wooden pagoda at Hwangnyong Monastery, and the holy belt. Kim Yul was familiar with the first two, but did not know about the third, the jade belt gifted by heaven to Silla king Chinp'yŏng (r. 579–632). The version of this story preserved in the *Memorabilia of the Three Kingdoms* suggests that Wang Kŏn believed that these three treasures functioned to confer legitimacy and protect the state from calamities, like the three treasures of the ancient Chinese Zhou dynasty (1046–256 BCE) – the Hall of Light (Mingtang), the imperial seal and the nine tripods. For this reason, he reportedly refrained from attacking Silla.

The Talgo, one of the Malgal tribes, crossed the borderlands into Sakchu prefecture looting villages and settlements in the second month of 921 – most likely because of their winter provisions being exhausted, and other chaos caused by the ongoing Khitan invasion of Parhae. The invaders were eradicated by Wang Kŏn's general and his troops garrisoned at Sakchu, and the Silla king, who still claimed suzerainty over the area, sent an official letter of gratitude to the Koryŏ king for protecting the people. Silla generals defending

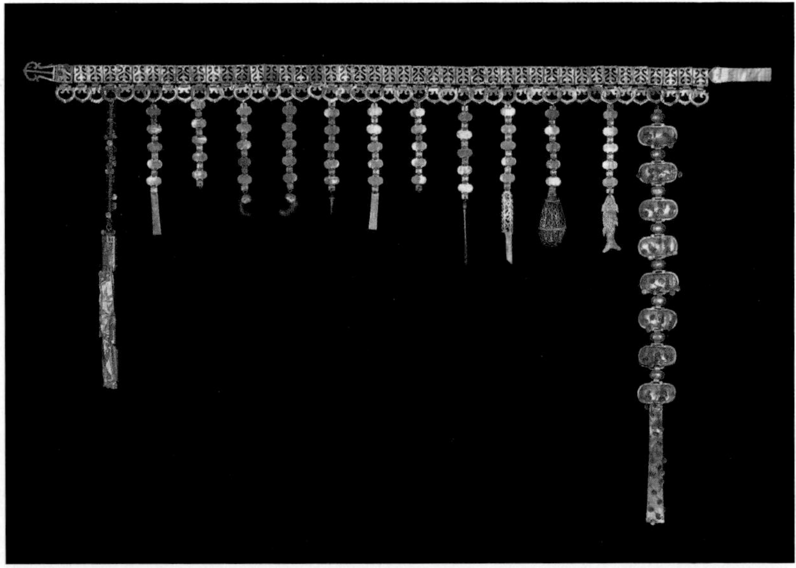

Gold belt, Silla, 6th century CE.

Wŏlchi, half-moon-shaped pond at Silla royal pleasure palace, Wŏlsŏng, Kyŏngju.

strategic strongholds on Silla's shrinking borders submitted to Wang Kŏn in 922 and 923. By 925, Silla was reduced to the area immediately surrounding the Silla capital, modern Kyŏngju. In the same year, the general of Koul superior prefecture, modern Yŏngch'ŏn in North Kyŏngsang province, submitted to Wang Kŏn. As this site was essentially the gateway to the Silla capital, he was praised by Wang and permitted to return to Silla.

After Later Paekche sacked the Silla capital in 927, Silla generals and administrative units continued to surrender to Koryŏ for protection against Kyŏn Hwŏn's depredations. The general of Chaeam Fortress submitted to Koryŏ in 930, and in the same year Wang Kŏn and Kyŏn Hwŏn battled south of Pyŏngsan in Koch'ang commandery, modern Andong in North Kyŏngsang province. More than thirty commanderies and districts surrendered to Wang Kŏn after Koryŏ's victory. To attend a summit meeting with Silla king Kyŏngsun on the political and social chaos induced by Kyŏn Hwŏn, Wang Kŏn journeyed to the Silla capital with an armed escort of fifty horsemen in 931. He returned with the Silla king's cousin as a hostage. In the eighth month of 931, by means of an envoy, the Koryŏ king gifted the Silla king with multicoloured silk and a horse saddle and presented bolts of silk and other precious cloth to Silla officials according to their ranks. More than thirty commanderies and districts in the area surrounding Unju, modern Hongsŏng in North Ch'ungch'ŏng province, surrendered to Wang Kŏn in the ninth month of 934.

In the tenth month of 935, Silla king Kyŏngsun recognized that his country could no longer defend itself adequately. Its once vast domain was broken and most of its surrounding districts and commanderies had yielded to Wang Kŏn or been conquered by Kyŏn Hwŏn. By means of a special envoy, he sent a letter to the Koryŏ king requesting to surrender. Wang Kŏn received the letter in the eleventh month and dispatched his high state councillor and others to welcome the Silla king. Kyŏngsun led his officials to Songak for the official ceremony, heading a convoy of carriages laden with treasures and beautiful women that extended for more than thirty *li*. Commoners lined the roads for a view of this once-in-a-lifetime spectacle. According to ritual propriety, Wang Kŏn waited for the Silla king in the suburbs of his capital city and lodged him in the noblest mansion east of the royal palace. Wang Kŏn formalized their relationship by marrying the former Silla king, Kim Pu, to his eldest daughter, the Princess Nangnang, and Wang Kŏn married Kim Pu's uncle's daughter, who became one of his queens. (She bore a son, posthumously titled Anjong (d. 996), who was the father of Koryŏ king Hyŏnjong (r. 1009–31).) Thereafter, the Koryŏ king invested him as Lord Chŏngsŭng, honouring him with a rank above that of the heir apparent. Wang Kŏn utilized the expertise of Silla officials, employing them in his government, and renamed the Silla capital Kyŏngju. Furthermore, he made Kyŏngju Kim Pu's emolument village. In the fifth month of 937, after Later Paekche's complete submission to Koryŏ rule in 935, Kim Pu reportedly presented the jade belt that heaven bestowed on Silla king Chinp'yŏng to Wang Kŏn, who accepted it and kept it safe in his treasury. Thus the Three Kingdoms period of Korean antiquity ended with the reunification of the peninsula under Koryŏ.

EPILOGUE

Although Koryŏ claimed to represent the re-establishment of Koguryŏ and derived symbolic authority from the ancient Korean state in Manchuria and the northern part of the Korean peninsula, the cultural legacy of Silla continued because the early Koryŏ state was profoundly influenced by the infusion of bureaucratic know-how from Silla, because it claimed to be the legitimate successor to Silla and because the Confucian and Buddhist traditions of the Greater Silla period continued on well into the Koryŏ period. The old Silla capital was renamed Kyŏngju and became the Eastern Capital of the Koryŏ state. In the late thirteenth century, during the age of Kublai Khan (r. 1260–94), the Koryŏ royal family even took up residence there while the country laboured to build its share of the armada that would so fatefully fail to subjugate the Japanese islands in 1274 and 1281. The Buddhist monk Iryŏn collected traditional narratives and other legends about Koguryŏ, Paekche, Kaya and Silla, as well as earlier polities, in his *Memorabilia of the Three Kingdoms* (*Samguk yusa*), but the lion's share of stories dealt with Silla.

During the succeeding Chosŏn period (1392–1910), Silla king T'aejong Muyŏl (Kim Ch'unch'u) was revered by Confucian scholars as an insightful ruler who understood the value of submitting to Tang China, adopting its refined culture and participating in the civilized Sinitic world. The Silla scholar-officials Sŏl Ch'ong and Ch'oe Ch'iwŏn were enshrined as the first two great Confucian

Seated stone Buddha, Maitreya Valley, Namsan, Kyŏngju, 8th century CE.

scholars of Korea in the Hall of Worthies (*chiphyŏn chŏn*). Stories of Silla figures were developed into novels in literary Sinitic, the lingua franca of the educated elite in East Asia, and circulated in both handwritten manuscripts and woodblock prints in the late Chosŏn period. *The Tale of Lone Cloud Ch'oe* (*Ch'oe Koun chŏn*), for instance, is a Confucian-inspired fantasy novel portraying Ch'oe Ch'iwŏn as a gifted youth who saves Silla through his extraordinary skills and abilities in poetic composition. Due to the relative wealth of narratives and legends about the life of the Silla general and statesman Kim Yusin, including a lengthy official biography in the *History of the Three Kingdoms*, several novels were created about him in the late Chosŏn period and early modern era – in the late nineteenth and early twentieth centuries – including the *Romance of King Hŭngmu* (*Hŭngmuwang yŏnŭi*), the *Veritable Record of King Hŭngmu* (*Hŭngmuwang silgi*) and the *Veritable Record of Master Kakkan* (*Kakkan sŏnsaeng silgi*). Although most were written in literary Sinitic, a few circulated in versions featuring mixed Chinese with Korean script, the *Tale of King Hŭngmu* (*Hŭngmuwang chŏn*), and in Korean script only, the *Veritable Record of Kim Yusin* (*Kim Yusin silgŭi*).

In the early twentieth century, some educated Koreans began to wonder about the cost of Korea's long-inherited obsession with Chinese culture after the floundering Qing dynasty (1644–1911) suffered a series of embarrassing defeats first by Western powers and then by the newly modernizing Japan in the Sino-Japanese War of 1894–5. After Korea became a protectorate of Japan in 1905 and before it became a colony in 1910, young Korean scholars and historians began to rethink their country's relationship with China and Chinese culture, and writers and artists mined Koguryŏ and Parhae history for new nationalistic heroes, such as Sin Ch'aeho's (1880–1936) exposition *Ŭlchi Mundŏk* (1908), which asserted that the Koguryŏ general famous for the stunning Koguryŏ victory over the Sui expeditionary force in 612 was more appropriately a patriotic warrior than was Kim Yusin. However, during the colonial period (1910–45), Japanese interest in the historical remains of Silla in Kyŏngju and surrounding North Kyŏngsang province reawakened the attention of many Korean scholars regarding Silla history

East and west pagodas of Kamŭn Monastery, the votive temple of Silla king Munmu, Kyŏngju, *c.* 682.

and culture. Of particular interest were exquisite gold crowns and other artefacts excavated from Silla royal tombs; the high level of mathematics, technology and craftsmanship seen in the granite cave shrine of Sŏkkuram; the rediscovery of native songs (*hyangga*) and early Korean literature; and the *hwarang*.

Due to the division of Korea at the 38th parallel, and the Cold War, the Silla contribution to traditional Korean culture continued to be emphasized by both the Korean government and scholars. With the growing economic success of Korea, many young Koreans in the late twentieth century began to wonder how Korean history would have been different had Koguryŏ and not Silla 'unified' the Three Kingdoms. The Northeast Project of the Chinese Academy of Social Sciences, which lasted from 2002 to 2007, recast the ancient kingdom of Koguryŏ as a 'local ethnic minority state' in the context of Chinese history as opposed to Korean history. This spurred a fervent response by the Republic of Korea in the creation of the Northeast Asia History Foundation in 2006. One of its primary objectives is to emphasize the centrality of Koguryŏ to Korean history. General Korean interest in Koguryŏ and Parhae has increased manyfold since the late twentieth century. Popular passion for Parhae is exemplified in the rock group Seo Taeji and the Boys' song 'Parhae rŭl kkumkkumyŏ' (Dreaming of Parhae) (1994) and the Korean martial arts fantasy film *The Legend of the Shadowless Sword* (2005).

REFERENCES

1 Wang Chong, *Lunheng jiaoshi* (*Doctrines Evaluated*), ed. Huang Hui (Beijing, 1996), pp. 81–2; translation following Kenneth H. J. Gardiner, 'The Legends of Koguryŏ (II)', *Korea Journal*, XXII/2 (February 1982), pp. 31–48, esp. 31–2.

2 Peter H. Lee and Wm Theodore de Bary, eds, *Sources of Korean Tradition*, vol. I: *From Early Times to the Sixteenth Century* (New York, 1997), p. 24.

3 Kim Pusik, *Samguk sagi* (*History of the Three Kingdoms*), 50 rolls, ed. Chŏng Kubok et al. (Seoul, 1996), roll 23, p. 224; cf. Jonathan W. Best, *A History of the Early Korean Kingdom of Paekche: Together with an Annotated Translation of the Paekche Annals of the Samguk Sagi* (Cambridge, MA, 2006), pp. 205–7.

4 Kim Pusik, *Samguk sagi*, roll 23, pp. 224–5; cf. Best, *A History of the Early Korean Kingdom of Paekche*, pp. 208–10.

5 Iryŏn, *Samguk yusa* (*Memorabilia of the Three Kingdoms*), 5 rolls, ed. Ch'oe Namsŏn (Seoul, 1954), roll 2, p. 98.

6 Wei Zheng et al., *Sui shu* (*History of the Sui*), 85 rolls, 6 vols (Beijing, 1973), roll 60, p. 1455; roll 61, p. 1466; and roll 63, pp. 1500–1501; Kim Pusik, *Samguk sagi*, roll 44, p. 422.

7 Chen Shou, comp., *Sanguo zhi* (*Monograph on the Three Kingdoms*), 65 rolls, 3 vols (Beijing, 1962), roll 30, p. 852.

8 Kim Pusik, *Samguk sagi*, roll 7, p. 85 (Munmu 11).

9 Ouyang Xiu, Song Qi et al., comp., *Xin Tang shu* (*New History of the Tang*), 225 rolls, 20 vols (Beijing, 1975), roll 220, p. 6202.

10 Liu Xu et al., comp., *Jiu Tang shu* (*Old History of the Tang*), 200 rolls, 16 vols (Beijing, 1975), roll 199A, p. 5334.

11 Liu Xu, *Jiu Tang shu*, roll 199A, p. 5337.

12 Iryŏn, *Samguk yusa*, roll 5, p. 220.

13 Kim Pusik, *Samguk sagi*, roll 45, p. 433.

BIBLIOGRAPHY

SELECTED PRIMARY SOURCES

Chen Shou, comp., *Sanguo zhi* (*Monograph on the Three Kingdoms*), 65 rolls, 3 vols (Beijing, 1962)

Iryŏn, *Samguk yusa* (*Memorabilia of the Three Kingdoms*), 5 rolls, ed. Ch'oe Namsŏn (Seoul, 1954)

Kim Pusik, comp., *Samguk sagi* (*History of the Three Kingdoms*), 50 rolls, ed. Chŏng Kubok et al. (Seoul, 1996)

Liu Xu et al., comp., *Jiu Tang shu* (*Old History of the Tang*), 200 rolls, 16 vols (Beijing, 1975)

Ouyang Xiu, Song Qi et al., comp., *Xin Tang shu* (*New History of the Tang*), 225 rolls, 20 vols (Beijing, 1975)

Wang Chong, *Lunheng jiaoshi* (*Doctrines Evaluated*), ed. Huang Hui (Beijing, 1996)

Wei Zheng et al., *Sui shu* (*History of the Sui*), 85 rolls, 6 vols (Beijing, 1973)

GENERAL WORKS: THREE KINGDOMS

Lee Ki-baik, *A New History of Korea*, trans. Edward W. Wagner with Edward J. Shultz (Cambridge, MA, 1984)

Lee, Peter H., ed., *Sourcebook of Korean Civilization*, vol. I: *From Early Times to the Sixteenth Century* (New York, 1993)

Mohan, Pankaj N., ed., *The Ancient Korean Kingdom of Silla: Political Developments and Religious Ideology*, Societas Koreana Publication 1, 2nd edn (Seongnam-si, 2013)

INTRODUCTION

Gardiner, Kenneth H. J., 'The *Samguk sagi* and Its Sources', *Papers on Far Eastern History*, II (1970), pp. 1–42

McBride, Richard D., II, 'Is the *Samguk yusa* Reliable? Case Studies from Chinese and Korean Sources', *Journal of Korean Studies*, XI/1 (Fall 2006), pp. 163–89

—, 'Preserving the Lore of Korean Antiquity: An Introduction to Native and Local Sources in Iryŏn's *Samguk yusa*', *Acta Koreana*, x/2 (July 2007), pp. 1–38

Shultz, Edward J., 'An Introduction to the *Samguk sagi*', *Korean Studies*, XXVIII (2004), pp. 1–13

1 LEGENDS AND ORIGINS OF KOREA'S THREE KINGDOMS

Best, Jonathan W., *A History of the Early Korean Kingdom of Paekche: Together with an Annotated Translation of the Paekche Annals of the Samguk Sagi* (Cambridge, MA, 2006)

Gardiner, Kenneth H. J., *The Early History of Korea* (Honolulu, HI, 1969)

—, 'The Legends of Koguryŏ (I)', *Korea Journal*, XXII/1 (January 1982), pp. 60–69

—, 'The Legends of Koguryŏ (II)', *Korea Journal*, XXII/2 (February 1982), pp. 31–48

Lee, Peter H., and Wm Theodore de Bary, eds, *Sources of Korean Tradition*, vol. I: *From Early Times through the Sixteenth Century* (New York, 1997)

McBride, Richard D., II, 'Making and Remaking Silla Origins', *Journal of the American Oriental Society*, CXL/3 (2020), pp. 531–48

2 KOGURYŎ AND PAEKCHE

Best, Jonathan W., *A History of the Early Korean Kingdom of Paekche: Together with an Annotated Translation of the Paekche Annals of the Samguk Sagi* (Cambridge, MA, 2006)

Byington, Mark E., ed., *The History and Archeology of the Koguryŏ Kingdom*, Early Korea Project Occasional Series no. 4 (Cambridge, MA, 2016)

—, 'Koguryŏ State Formation and the Xuantu Commandery', in *The History and Archeology of the Koguryŏ Kingdom*, Early Korea Project Occasional Series, ed. Mark E. Byington (Cambridge, MA, 2016), pp. 31–70

Gabriel, Richard A., and Donald W. Boose, 'The Korean Way of War: Salsu River', in *The Great Battles of Antiquity: A Strategic and Tactical Guide to Great Battles That Shaped the Development of War*, ed. Richard A. Gabriel and Donald W. Boose (Westport, CT, 1994), pp. 461–87

No, T'ae-don, *Korea's Ancient Koguryŏ Kingdom: A Socio-Political History*, trans. John Huston (Leiden and Boston, MA, 2014)

Northeast Asian History Foundation, comp., *The Culture and Thought of Koguryŏ*, trans. Richard D. McBride II (Seoul, 2018)

Shultz, Edward J., and Hugh H. W. Kang, with Daniel C. Kane and Kenneth J. H. Gardiner, trans., *The Koguryŏ Annals of the* Samguk Sagi (Seongnam-si, 2011)

Yoshida Kazuhiko, 'The Credibility of the *Gangōji engi*', *Japanese Journal of Religious Studies*, XLII/1 (2015), pp. 89–107

3 KAYA AND EARLY SILLA

Lee, Soyoung, and Denise Patry Leidy, eds, *Silla: Korea's Golden Kingdom* (New York, 2014)
McBride, Richard D., II, 'Can the *Samguk sagi* Be Corroborated through Epigraphy? An Analysis of the Capital-Rank System and Councils of Nobles', *Seoul Journal of Korean Studies*, XXIX/1 (June 2016), pp. 65–91
—, 'The Evolution of Councils of Nobles in Silla Korea', *Tongguk sahak*, LIX (December 2015), pp. 263–318
—, 'Hidden Agendas in the Life Writings of Kim Yusin', *Acta Koreana*, I (August 1998), pp. 101–42
—, 'The Structure and Sources of the Biography of Kim Yusin', *Acta Koreana*, XVI/2 (December 2013), pp. 497–535
—, 'When Did the Rulers of Silla Become Kings?', *Han'guk kodaesa tamgu* (*Sogang Journal of Early Korean History*), VIII (August 2011), pp. 215–55
Shultz, Edward J., and Hugh H. W. Kang, with Daniel C. Kane, trans., *The Silla Annals of the* Samguk Sagi (Seongnam-si, 2012; rpt. 2017)

4 RELIGION AND CULTURE IN THE EARLY THREE KINGDOMS

McBride, Richard D., II, *Domesticating the Dharma: Buddhist Cults and the Hwaŏm Synthesis in Silla Korea* (Honolulu, HI, 2008)
—, 'Silla Buddhism and the Hwarang', *Korean Studies*, XXXIV (2010), pp. 54–89
—, 'The Vision-Quest Motif in Narrative Literature on the Buddhist Traditions of Silla', *Korean Studies*, XXVII (2003), pp. 16–47
—, 'What Is the Ancient Korean Religion?', *Acta Koreana*, IX/2 (July 2006), pp. 1–30
—, 'Yi Kyubo's Lay of the Old Shaman', in *Religions of Korea in Practice*, ed. Robert E. Buswell Jr (Princeton, NJ, 2007), pp. 233–43

5 GREATER SILLA AND PARHAE

Jamieson, John Charles, 'The *Samguk Sagi* and the Unification Wars', PhD Thesis, University of California, Berkeley, 1969
Lee, Soyoung, and Denise Patry Leidy, eds, *Silla: Korea's Golden Kingdom* (New York, 2014)
McBride, Richard D., II, 'King Sinmun's Symbolic Strengthening of Royal Authority: The Role of "The Royal Regulations" Chapter of the *Book of Rites* in the Mid-Silla Period', *Tongguk sahak*, LXVII (December 2019), pp. 115–67
—, 'Korea', in *A Companion to the Global Early Middle Ages*, ed. Erik Hermans (Leeds and Kalamazoo, MI, 2020), pp. 133–60
—, ed., *State and Society in Middle and Late Silla*, Early Korea Project Occasional Series no. 1 (Cambridge, MA, 2010)
Northeast Asian History Foundation, Seoul, comp., *A New History of Parhae*, trans. John Duncan (Leiden and Boston, MA, 2012)
Song Kiho, *The Clash of Histories in East Asia* (Seoul, 2010) (esp. pp. 273–404 on Parhae)

6 THE FLOURISHING OF BUDDHISM AND CONFUCIANISM IN GREATER SILLA

Buswell, Robert E., Jr, trans., *Cultivating Original Enlightenment: Wŏnhyo's Exposition of the* Vajrasamādhi-Sūtra *(Kŭmgang Sammae-gyŏng Non)*, Collected Works of Wŏnhyo, vol. I (Honolulu, HI, 2007)

—, *The Formation of Ch'an Ideology in China and Korea: The Vajrasamādhi-Sūtra, a Buddhist Apocryphon* (Princeton, NJ, 1989)

—, *Tracing Back the Radiance: Chinul's Korean Way of Zen* (Honolulu, HI, 1992)

Lee Hai-soon, 'Representation of Females in Twelfth-Century Korean Historiography', in *Women and Confucian Cultures in Premodern China, Korea, and Japan*, ed. Dorothy Ko, JaHyun Kim Haboush and Joan R. Piggot (Berkeley, Los Angeles and London, 2003), pp. 75–96

McBride, Richard D., II, *Aspiring to Enlightenment: Pure Land Buddhism in Silla Korea*, Pure Land Buddhist Studies Series (Honolulu, HI, 2020)

—, 'Buddhist Kingship and Symbolic Architecture in Silla Korea', *International Journal of Buddhist Thought and Culture*, XXXI/1 (June 2021), pp. 181–215

—, *Domesticating the Dharma: Buddhist Cults and the Hwaŏm Synthesis in Silla Korea* (Honolulu, HI, 2008)

—, ed., *Hwaŏm I: The Mainstream Tradition*, Collected Works of Korean Buddhism, vol. IV, trans. Richard D. McBride II and Sem Vermeersch (Seoul, 2012)

—, ed., *Hwaŏm II: Selected Works*, Collected Works of Korean Buddhism, vol. V, trans. Richard D. McBride II (Seoul, 2012)

—, 'Korea', in *A Companion to the Global Early Middle Ages*, ed. Erik Hermans (Leeds and Kalamazoo, MI, 2020), pp. 133–60

—, 'A Miraculous Tale of Buddhist Practice in Unified Silla', in *Religions of Korea in Practice*, ed. Robert E. Buswell Jr (Princeton, NJ, 2007), pp. 65–75

—, 'Of Monasteries and Monks: Mainstream Sinitic Buddhism in the Poetry of Ch'oe Ch'iwŏn', *Acta Koreana*, XXIV/1 (June 2021), pp. 1–30

—, ed. *State and Society in Middle and Late Silla*, Early Korea Project Occasional Series no. 1 (Cambridge, MA, 2010)

7 THE GOOD, THE BAD AND THE UGLY IN THE LATER THREE KINGDOMS

Hurst, G. Cameron, '"The Good, the Bad and the Ugly": Personalities in the Founding of the Koryŏ Dynasty', *Korean Studies Forum*, VII (1981), pp. 1–27

McBride, Richard D., II, 'Blaming the Victim: Reconsidering Queen Chinsŏng and the Decline of Silla', *Tongguk sahak*, LXIX (December 2020), pp. 603–49

—, 'Why Did Kungye Claim to Be the Buddha Maitreya? The Maitreya Cult and Royal Power in the Silla–Koryŏ Transition', *Journal of Inner and East Asian Studies*, II/1 (2004), pp. 37–62

PHOTO ACKNOWLEDGEMENTS

The author and publishers wish to express their thanks to the sources listed below for illustrative material and/or permission to reproduce it. Some locations of artworks are also given below, in the interest of brevity:

Photo Mark E. Byington: p. 29; Cultural Heritage Administration, Daejeon (Korea Open Government License): pp. 41, 68 (Buyeo (Puyŏ) National Museum), 98, 105 (Buyeo (Puyŏ) National Museum), 126, 127, 147, 152 (National Museum of Korea, Seoul), 156, 158, 186 (National Museum of Korea, Seoul), 199; EDU Vision/ Alamy Stock Photo: p. 64; Gyeongju (Kyŏngju) National Museum (Korea Open Government License): pp. 30, 38–9, 40, 43, 76, 79, 82, 92, 106, 119, 133, 135, 137, 142, 150, 167, 173, 176, 180, 184, 188, 192; Isonokami Shrine, Nara, photo Buyeo (Puyŏ) National Museum (Korea Open Government License): p. 52; photos Richard D. McBride II: pp. 131, 139, 154, 160, 171, 181, 190, 196; National Museum of Korea, Seoul (Korea Open Government License): pp. 24, 25, 26, 33, 48, 49, 55, 60, 61, 70, 73, 83, 84, 88, 99, 102, 108, 114, 115, 116, 144; National Palace Museum, Taipei: pp. 56, 57, 87; Qianling Mausoleum, near Xi'an: p. 123; Stock for you/Shutterstock.com: p. 193; courtesy ThinkSpatial, BYU Geography, Provo, UT: pp. 18, 120.

INDEX

Page numbers in *italics* refer to illustrations